Test-Driven Development with Django

Develop powerful, fully-featured Django applications by writing tests first

Kevin Harvey

PUBLISHING

BIRMINGHAM - MUMBAI

Test-Driven Development with Django

First published: July 2015

Production reference: 1230715

Published by Packt Publishing Ltd.
Livery Place
35 Livery Street
Birmingham B3 2PB, UK.

ISBN 978-1-78528-116-7

www.packtpub.com

Credits

Author
Kevin Harvey

Reviewers
Ian Cordasco
Anamta Farook
Jason Myers
Vimal Atreya Ramaka
Yogendra Sharma

Commissioning Editor
Ashwin Nair

Acquisition Editor
Shaon Basu

Content Development Editor
Susmita Sabat

Technical Editors
Prajakta Mhatre
Manan Patel

Copy Editor
Yesha Gangani

Project Coordinator
Milton Dsouza

Proofreader
Safis Editing

Indexer
Rekha Nair

Production Coordinator
Melwyn D'sa

Cover Work
Melwyn D'sa

About the Author

Kevin Harvey first fell in love with Django while living in Quelimane, Mozambique, in 2007. His professional interests include software quality, open source, and teaching. He continues to be amazed at the Python community's ability to turn a history major into a software engineer, a feat for which he will forever be indebted. When not writing unit tests, Kevin enjoys playing the bass (both electric and stand up), and cooking with entirely too much butter. He lives in Nashville, Tennessee, with his wife and their two sons.

There are many without whom this book would not have been possible. My thanks go to: Michael Trachtman, for helping me hash out my thoughts on the subject over the last 3 years; Julie Barnick, for helping me apply theory to the real world; Nate Aune, for his continued guidance; John Roth, for his enthusiasm; Medora Willmore, for teaching me how to write; Joe Killian, for encouraging me to write; Eli Bortz, for his industry advice; Jason Myers, for his unlimited willingness to help others; and finally, my wife Lara, for providing useful feedback on a topic that she knows nothing about, and dealing with the twins while daddy worked on his book.

About the Reviewers

Ian Cordasco is a core developer of requests, Flake8, Twine, Betamax, Chardet, and github3.py, as well as a core reviewer and driver for multiple OpenStack projects. As a polyglot, Ian frequently borrows testing ideas from other languages to improve the quality of Python's testing ecosystem.

Anamta Farook is a software developer with a unique background in education and design. She graduated from Brown University in 2014 and has been programming professionally for the past year. Anamta enjoys working at trailblazing startups; she is currently employed at Maxwell Health, and she previously worked at Coursolve. She has 10 years of experience in teaching and developing educational content. She is particularly passionate about opportunities at the nexus of education and computer science, such as reviewing this book!

> I'd like to thank my parents, who encouraged me to take on this challenge. It's been a fun experience and I've really enjoyed being the voice of the learner in this book. I am confident that our readers will find this book an easy, valuable guide to Test-Driven Development.

Jason Myers works at Cisco as a software engineer, working on OpenStack. Prior to switching to development a few years ago, he spent 15 years as a systems architect, and has build data centers and cloud architectures for several of the largest tech companies, hospitals, stadiums, and telecomm providers. He's a passionate developer who regularly speaks at local and national events about technology. He's also the chair of the PyTennessee conference. He loves solving human problems, and has a side project, Sucratrend, which is devoted to helping diabetics manage their condition and improve their quality of life. He has used SQLAlchemy in web, data warehouse, and analytics applications, and is currently writing *Essential SQLAlchemy*, 2nd Edition.

Vimal Atreya Ramaka has graduated from the University of Prince Edward Island in computer science and business administration, and after graduation, she has started working as the tech lead for Climate Research Lab at the University of Prince Edward Island. Her domain is located at `http://vimal.ramaka.com`.

Yogendra Sharma works at Siemens Industry Software Pvt. Ltd as a product developer and lives in Pune. He is a gold medalist in post graduation diploma. The course that he has graduated in is advance computing from CDAC, and he has also completed his bachelor's of technology in computer science. He is basically an engineer by heart and a technical enthusiast by nature.

He has vast experience in the fields of C++, Python, Django, Java, J2EE technologies, and Web App Security.

Yogendra was also the technical reviewer of *Mastering Python Design Patterns*, published by Packt Publishing.

You can find him on LinkedIn at `http://in.linkedin.com/in/yogendra0sharma`. You can also visit `http://PyLabs.in`.

I would like to thank my father for allowing me to learn all that I did. I would also like to thank my friends for their support and encouragement.

www.PacktPub.com

Support files, eBooks, discount offers, and more

For support files and downloads related to your book, please visit www.PacktPub.com.

Did you know that Packt offers eBook versions of every book published, with PDF and ePub files available? You can upgrade to the eBook version at www.PacktPub.com and as a print book customer, you are entitled to a discount on the eBook copy. Get in touch with us at service@packtpub.com for more details.

At www.PacktPub.com, you can also read a collection of free technical articles, sign up for a range of free newsletters and receive exclusive discounts and offers on Packt books and eBooks.

https://www2.packtpub.com/books/subscription/packtlib

Do you need instant solutions to your IT questions? PacktLib is Packt's online digital book library. Here, you can search, access, and read Packt's entire library of books.

Why subscribe?

- Fully searchable across every book published by Packt
- Copy and paste, print, and bookmark content
- On demand and accessible via a web browser

Free access for Packt account holders

If you have an account with Packt at www.PacktPub.com, you can use this to access PacktLib today and view 9 entirely free books. Simply use your login credentials for immediate access.

This book is dedicated to Dr. Eric-Jan Manders. Eric, thanks for showing me the path.

Table of Contents

Preface

Writing software is hard. Even the smallest projects have many moving parts. We developers are not only expected to get those parts moving, but keep them moving as the application changes over time. Test-Driven Development (TDD) is a methodology that allows us to quantify the successful function of each of these parts before we attempt to code them. Using TDD, we can focus on a single part of the application at a time, leaving a trail of tests that guard against regression as we continue to update the application.

Django is a popular web framework written in Python. Its batteries-included: the framework itself includes URL routing, object-relational mapping, templates, and many other necessities for building a modern web application. This book will take you through the process of developing a Django app by writing failing tests first, then writing application code to make those tests pass.

What this book covers

Chapter 1, *Keeping Your Promises*, describes the benefits of TDD in comparison to other styles of programming. We'll look at a very simple example, and talk about testing as a pillar of professional software development.

Chapter 2, *Your First Test-Driven Application*, introduces the example application that we'll be building throughout the book. We'll translate a user story into a browser-based functional test using Selenium, and write unit tests and application code to start to fulfill that user story.

Chapter 3, *Ironclad Code*, continues where the previous chapter left off, digging deeper into the API available for writing unit tests in Django. We'll cover the Python Debugger, RequestFactory, and TestClient, among other tools.

Chapter 4, *Building Out and Refactoring*, adds new features to the application. We'll use our test suite to maintain existing functionality while refactoring to keep our code tidy and maintainable.

Chapter 5, *User Stories As Code*, focuses on LiveServerTestCase and the Python Selenium bindings we use to drive the browser during a test run. We'll learn how to select and click on elements, submit forms, switch between open windows, and perform other user actions in our UI.

Chapter 6, *No App Is an Island*, applies the TDD methodology to third-party API integration. We'll learn when, why, and how to mock out HTTP requests inside a single unit test so that our tests aren't relying on an outside resource (even if our app is).

Chapter 7, *Share and Share Alike*, introduces Django REST Framework—a tool for building a REST API with Django. We'll cover the importance of documentation when writing an API, and use the framework's tools to send requests to the API during tests.

Chapter 8, *Promises Kept*, takes a look back at what we've learned, and whether we've realized all the benefits from the first chapter. We'll get suggestions for next steps in TDD, and talk about some of the common pitfalls you may encounter.

What you need for this book

In order to follow along with the examples in this book, you'll need a computer with a command line interface (the default is Terminal for Linux and Mac, and Command Prompt for Windows) with Python installed. You will also need an Internet connection to download third-party packages and a text editor for writing Python code.

Who this book is for

This book is for Django developers who want to learn about TDD, and how it might help them in their work. It's expected that the reader is comfortable with reading and writing Python and has some familiarity with the Django framework.

Conventions

In this book, you will find a number of text styles that distinguish between different kinds of information. Here are some examples of these styles and an explanation of their meaning.

Code words in text, database table names, folder names, filenames, file extensions, pathnames, dummy URLs, user input, and Twitter handles are shown as follows: "If you're making HTTP calls, the `requests` package is a great option."

A block of code is set as follows:

```
# multiplicator.py
defmultiplicator(x, y):
    pass
```

Any command-line input or output is written as follows:

```
$ python
>>> from multiplicator import multiplicator
>>>multiplicator(2, 3)
6
```

New terms and **important words** are shown in bold, like this: " A **Continuous Integration (CI)** server, for our purposes, can pull our project from version control "

Reader feedback

Feedback from our readers is always welcome. Let us know what you think about this book—what you liked or disliked. Reader feedback is important for us as it helps us develop titles that you will really get the most out of.

To send us general feedback, simply e-mail feedback@packtpub.com, and mention the book's title in the subject of your message.

If there is a topic that you have expertise in and you are interested in either writing or contributing to a book, see our author guide at www.packtpub.com/authors.

Customer support

Now that you are the proud owner of a Packt book, we have a number of things to help you to get the most from your purchase.

Downloading the example code

You can download the example code files from your account at http://www.packtpub.com for all the Packt Publishing books you have purchased. If you purchased this book elsewhere, you can visit http://www.packtpub.com/support and register to have the files e-mailed directly to you.

The source code for the sample application is available on GitHub at `https://github.com/kevinharvey/jmad` on the `test-driven-django-development` branch (the repository's default). Development milestones in the book have been tagged with names like `ch5-2-staff-login` to make navigating the repository easier.

Errata

Although we have taken every care to ensure the accuracy of our content, mistakes do happen. If you find a mistake in one of our books—maybe a mistake in the text or the code—we would be grateful if you could report this to us. By doing so, you can save other readers from frustration and help us improve subsequent versions of this book. If you find any errata, please report them by visiting `http://www.packtpub.com/submit-errata`, selecting your book, clicking on the **Errata Submission Form** link, and entering the details of your errata. Once your errata are verified, your submission will be accepted and the errata will be uploaded to our website or added to any list of existing errata under the Errata section of that title.

To view the previously submitted errata, go to `https://www.packtpub.com/books/content/support` and enter the name of the book in the search field. The required information will appear under the **Errata** section.

Piracy

Piracy of copyrighted material on the Internet is an ongoing problem across all media. At Packt, we take the protection of our copyright and licenses very seriously. If you come across any illegal copies of our works in any form on the Internet, please provide us with the location address or website name immediately so that we can pursue a remedy.

Please contact us at `copyright@packtpub.com` with a link to the suspected pirated material.

We appreciate your help in protecting our authors and our ability to bring you valuable content.

Questions

If you have a problem with any aspect of this book, you can contact us at `questions@packtpub.com`, and we will do our best to address the problem.

1
Keeping Your Promises

In this chapter, we'll be introduced to Test-Driven Development. We will explore:

- What is Test-Driven Development?
- How does Test-Driven Development help build better software?
- Doesn't it take longer?
- Can't I just write the tests later?

What is Test-Driven Development?

Test-Driven Development (TDD) is the practice of:

1. writing a deliberately failing test,
2. writing application code to make the test pass,
3. refactoring to optimize the code while the test continues to pass, and
4. repeating the process until your project is complete.

The initial test is the bar you set for the logic that you want to write. It's a great way to ensure that your tests cover every nook and cranny of your code, and that it delivers exactly what you said it would.

Throughout this book, we'll explore TDD through numerous examples in a medium-sized Django project. We'll use lots of different Python utilities and see lots of sample code. The takeaway should not be any particular package (there are many other tools besides the ones we'll feature in this book), but the process itself and the change in approach required. It's a methodology, not a technology. It's a way of building applications and a discipline that requires practice.

A simple example

Here's a quick example using Python's built-in `assert`, a statement that evaluates a condition. It will throw an `AssertionError` if the condition is false, and returns nothing otherwise.

Let's say we wanted a Python function that could multiply two numbers together and return the result. Let's call it `multiplicator`.

The first step in TDD, before writing any code, is to find a way to test the application you want to write. If you're having trouble coming up with a test scenario, imagine that you've already written the application (in this case, that single function) and want to try it out in the command line. You'd probably do something like this:

```
$ python
>>> from multiplicator import multiplicator
>>> multiplicator(2, 3)
6
```

You, the human, would look at the output of the function call (6) and confirm that the operation was performed successfully. How can we teach our application to do this confirmation itself? Enter `assert`. Create a file called `multiplicator.py` and enter the following code:

```
# multiplicator.py
assert multiplicator(2, 3) == 6
```

We can translate this statement into English as "run `multiplicator` with arguments 2 and 3 and throw an error if the returned value does not equal 6."

 We'll get into the more interesting tools available in the `unittest` library in *Chapter 2, Your First Test-Driven Application*. For now, this is all we need to see how TDD works.

We now have a runnable test for our function, without so much as an attempt to write the function itself. Let's run it and see what happens:

```
$ python multiplicator.py
Traceback (most recent call last):
  File "multiplicator.py", line 1, in <module>
    assert multiplicator(2, 3) == 6
NameError: name 'multiplicator' is not defined
```

Looks like Python can't find anything called `multiplicator`. We can fix that with the following code:

```python
# multiplicator.py
def multiplicator():
    pass


assert multiplicator(2,3) == 6
```

Try running the test now:

```
$ python multiplicator.py
Traceback (most recent call last):
  File "multiplicator.py", line 4, in <module>
    assert multiplicator(2, 3) == 6
TypeError: multiplicator() takes 0 positional arguments but 2 were
given
```

Okay, our function needs to accept some arguments. Let's update it:

```python
# multiplicator.py
def multiplicator(x, y):
    pass


assert multiplicator(2, 3) == 6
```

And finally, when we run our test again:

```
$ python multiplicator.py
Traceback (most recent call last):
  File "multiplicator.py", line 4, in <module>
    assert multiplicator(2, 3) == 6
AssertionError
```

This `AssertionError` is the one we asked our test to throw (via `assert`) if the result of our function did not equal the expected value (6). Now that we're here, we can write some logic:

```python
# multiplicator.py
def multiplicator(x, y):
    i = 0
    result = 0
    while i < x:
        result += y
        i += 1
```

```
    return result

assert multiplicator(2, 3) == 6
```

Whoa there, Tex! That's one way to do it… I suppose. Should we run the tests?

```
$ python multiplicator.py
```

Huh? No output? No error? You mean that monstrosity actually made the test pass?

Yes it did! We wrote application code to make the test pass without any pressure to optimize it, or without picking *the best* Python function to make it work. Now that we have the test passing, we can optimize to our heart's content; we know we're safe as long as the test continues to pass.

Let's update `multiplicator` to use some of Python's own integer arithmetic:

```
# multiplicator.py
def multiplicator(x, y):
    return x*y

assert multiplicator(2, 3) == 6
```

Now, we can run our test again:

```
$ python multiplicator.py
```

That's better. We built a working, optimized function and a test suite to check for regressions using basic TDD methodology. This process is often referred to as "red/green/refactor".

Red/green/refactor

The smallest cycle of TDD typically involves three steps:

1. Writing a test that fails (red).
2. Doing whatever is necessary to get that test to pass (green).
3. Optimizing to fix any subpar code you may have introduced to get the test to pass (refactor).

In the preceding example, we wrote a test for the desired functionality and watched it fail (red). Then we wrote some less-than-optimal code to get it to pass (green). Finally, we refactored the code to simplify the logic while keeping the test passing (refactor). This virtuous circle is how TDD helps you write code that is both functional and beautiful.

Testing is a pillar of professional software development

There are four key practices to writing great code:

1. Version control
2. Documentation
3. Testing
4. Continuous Integration

Each builds upon the next and a thoughtful execution of each guarantees the delivery of quality software.

Version control

Version control is the ultimate undo button. It allows you to check code changes into a repository at regular intervals and rollback to any of those changes later. We'll be using Git throughout the course of this book. To get a good primer on Git, check out `http://git-scm.com/doc`.

Documentation

If we're using TDD to keep promises, documentation is where we first make these promises. Simply put, documentation describes how your application works. At a minimum, your software project needs the development documentation for the next person to maintain it (even if it's you, you'll forget what you wrote). You'll probably need some less technical documentation for the end user as well.

Testing

Testing and documentation have a crucial relationship—your tests prove that your documentation is telling the truth. For instance, the documentation for a REST API may instruct a developer to send a POST request to a given URL, with a certain JSON payload in order to get back a certain response. You can ensure this is what happens by exercising this specific behavior in your tests.

Continuous Integration

All of these glorious tests will be pretty useless if no one is running them. Luckily, actually running the tests (and alerting us of any failures) is another thing we can train a machine to do. A **Continuous Integration** (**CI**) server, for our purposes, can pull our project from version control, build it, run our tests, and alert us if any errors or failures occur. It can also be the first place where our tests are run in a production-like environment (for instance, in the same operating system and database configuration), allowing us to keep our local environments configured for speed and ease.

How does TDD help in building better software?

From the outset, Test-Driven Development seems like a lot more work. We could very well be doubling the size of our code base with a test for every single branch in our logic. Here's why all that extra code will be worth it:

- **It will keep you on track**: Writing the tests first is like keeping an executable checklist of all the development tasks you have to complete. Good functional tests are the key link between user stories (which is what everyone really cares about) and your code. A well-designed functional test will ensure that the end user will be able to do everything they need to do with your application.

- **You will build exactly (and only) what is required**: As we'll see in *Chapter 2, Your First Test-Driven Application*, a good first step in Test-Driven Development is the translation of a user story into a distinct, self-contained functional test. Codifying the project's requirements as a test and *only writing enough code to make that test pass* will ensure that you've fulfilled all the user stories and guard against any scope creep. The project itself will help you determine when development is complete, or if any changes introduced later would interfere with any end-user functionality.

- **You're teaching your application to check itself**: Humans are better at computers in lots of ways, but the silicon has us beat when it comes to proofreading code. All we have to do is teach the machines what to look for by writing tests. Then, we can send them scampering through our files, confirming every function output, and checking every attribute of every class, any time we want.

- **It will help clarify your thinking**: Computer applications are abstract models of real-world systems that solve problems for human beings. Abstracting solutions to human problems in computer code takes serious thought and care. By clearly defining the functionality of your application with a test before you try to develop it, you force yourself to program with the end goal in mind. Having laid out the *meaning* of the application in a functional test (even if it's just stubbed out) helps to keep you on target even when you're elbow-deep in the logic.

- **Post-development tests just don't have the same weight**: If you try to write a test for some code that already does what you want, you'd have already closed your mind to the other possibilities of that code. You'll wind up with a narrow test that only covers that aspect of the code that you were thinking about while you were writing it. Writing the test when you're free of any preconceptions will yield a test that's more comprehensive, which will in turn produce stronger, less buggy code.

- **You will achieve flow**: TDD is all about incremental improvement. Each new test that passes (or incremental step to get to the next error in a test) is a little win. Plus, you won't have to spend hours debugging if you mess something up and a test fails. You'll be able to go right to the problem because the test that you wrote before you built that part of the application will be the one that failed.

  Have you ever worked on a project where considerable effort went into maintaining a "development" database? Maybe it was set up so that you could check the effect of a custom `save` method from time to time? Or maybe you needed to dive into `./manage.py shell`, import a bunch of your code, instantiate a few models, and then run your method to see if it worked? There's no monkey business like this when you write the tests first. The application state that you need is codified in your test suite. All that set up will happen in one command and on every run (not just when you're futzing with that method).

- **No one will ever know how buggy your code started out**: If you've worked on software projects of any complexity, you've probably developed a healthy fear of change. Change breaks stuff, particularly change to a part of an application that finds itself imported all over your project. However, if you've developed the entire application writing tests first, you've left a trail of test coverage that will alert you well before that bug you just wrote gets in to source control, let alone deployed. TDD allows you to refactor and optimize without fear of regression.

- **Bugs will stay fixed**: If I write a failing test that demonstrates a bug report that I receive, then update my application to make the test pass, I'll never have to worry about that bug coming back ever again because my test will catch it. Less time worrying about my production application means more fearless feature development.

- **You'll work better with your team**: An important part of working in a development team is explaining the code you write to your fellow developers. There's no better way to explain your code than to walk through your tests. Better yet, write tests as a team to foster collaboration and keep everyone on the same page.

- **You'll write testable code**: Code that is easily tested is better code. It seems both silly and obvious but it's worth mentioning. If you can prove beyond a shadow of a doubt that your code has the desired effect or return value, you'll be better able to maintain it. Writing the test before you write the code will force you to write code that can be easily tested.

- **You'll achieve the impossible**: There is nothing like a blank-slate TDD project to make you feel like you can save the world. When there is not even a hint of a function yet, you can assert any return value or effect you can imagine with any input you want. Don't hold back just because you have no idea how to build a function that would satisfy the pie-in-the-sky test you wrote. Write the test, hack away until you get it to pass, and then clean up your mess with a refactor.

```
def get_the_answer_to_the_ultimate_question():
    # TODO: ask Mr. Dent
    pass

assert get_the_answer_to_the_ultimate_question() == 42
```

Test-Driven Deep Thought Development

- **You'll be able to take big risks**: We've all been there—late in the development process or even after shipment, we see a tweak that we'd like to make in a linchpin model or method. The tweak would be a tremendous boon to system performance, but the change would have an unknown effect on nearly every other part of the application. If we've followed TDD, we'll have a complete test suite that will allow us to know the ramifications of that change immediately. We'll be able to make the change, run the tests, and see early on what it would take to keep the rest of the system in place.

- **You'll look like a pro**: When you release your code out into the world, either as a user-facing application or an installable package for other developers, you're making a promise to the people that use it. You're promising that the documentation was in fact accurate and that the dang thing does what it's supposed to do. A comprehensive test suite helps keep that promise and there's no better way to build one than by following the TDD mantra.

  Particularly in the open source world, the presence of a test suite lets the community know that you're serious. It's the first thing you should look for when evaluating a new PyPI package to install. A test suite says that you can trust this software.

Doesn't it take longer?

A common criticism of TDD is that it slows down the development cycle. All these tests are a bunch more code. Wouldn't you have to go back and update them if you changed your application?

The answer is yes, in the short term, TDD will add time to the development cycle, particularly when you're first learning it. Writing tests is a skill and skills take practice. Once you're through the learning curve, writing test functions is much easier and faster than writing the application code. Tests are generally terse (do this, do this, check that, and so on) without complicated logic or looping. The best tests are the simplest ones. You'll be able to crank them out quickly.

The extra effort in TDD comes with the added thinking you have to do. Writing a test before you write code requires a true understanding of what you're trying to accomplish, which can be hard. But does that honestly sound like a bad thing? I'd argue that this is a decidedly positive aspect of TDD—added time spent thinking through the meaning of your code yields higher quality code. You'll uncover unforeseen complications as your tests reveal edge cases that didn't come out in code review sessions. Conversations with project owners will be more meaningful after you've put the requirements through their paces. Your application code will benefit from the extra care.

Now let's talk about the long term. Towards the end of the project, or even after launch, a big change will come down from the product owner (this is Agile, right?) or you'll find something fundamental that you want to modify. The comprehensive test suite you've built through TDD will pay you back in spades when something goes wrong, or if you need to refactor. The flexibility provided by your test suite will likely save you more time than you spent creating it. You'll thank TDD in the end.

Can't I just write the tests later?

There are many reasons that you may want to develop without writing tests first. Maybe you're using a new API and can't begin to think about how to write tests. Maybe you want to build a simple application quickly as a proof of concept for a client.

By all means, write code without tests, but know that *code without tests is a prototype at best*. Resist the urge to start the production version of your project from a testless prototype. After prototyping, start again with TDD instead of trying to go back, and write tests for the prototype.

Even if you are only creating a prototype, consider TDD for any complexity at all. If you find yourself repeatedly dropping into `./manage.py shell` sessions to set up, execute, and evaluate a function under development, write a test or two to turn that process into a single command.

Summary

In this chapter, we introduced the practice of TDD and the benefits of using it. In the next chapter, we will start a Django project from scratch using rigorous TDD methodology, learning some of the testing tools available in Django and Python along the way.

2
Your First Test-Driven Application

In this chapter, we will start a new web application from the ground up by writing tests first. To do that, we will:

- Learn the difference between functional tests and unit tests, and when to use each
- Gather requirements for the application that we're going to build, including a user story and acceptance criteria
- Learn the basics of the testing APIs available in a Django project

Where do we begin?

We'll get to the code soon enough, but there is work to be done before anything is committed to the repository. Test-Driven Development (TDD) starts the way you'd expect—with requirements gathering. We'll write our requirements as user stories with acceptance criteria, and those user stories will be translated into functional tests. Functional tests will help us write unit tests, which will in turn lead to application code.

I encourage you to follow along with the examples by typing them directly into your command line and text editor. TDD is all about establishing a flow, and you can't establish a flow by copying and pasting.

Functional versus unit tests

There are many ways to describe types of tests. For our purposes, we will differentiate between unit tests and functional tests. The distinction is semantic but will inform our testing strategy.

User versus developer experience

When writing tests, we're speaking to someone else about our code. The type of test that we're writing is determined by our audience. Functional tests are wholly focused on the user experience. They ensure that the sum total of data and logic in your application add up to the functionality that you've promised your users.

Alternatively, unit tests typically focus on concerns of the developer. They often answer the question, "If I run function x with input y, do I get output z as expected?" Users don't care about the nitty-gritty details such as this, but developers do.

Size

Unit tests are usually tiny, sometimes as small as a single line of code. They run in microseconds. They're typically written to test a single, atomic part of the project, so their failure typically indicates an error in a distinct area in an application.

Functional tests can be *big*, running through an application just as a normal user would. This means that they can take a long time to run, and that they depend on a lot of the code to work. A failure in a functional test can sometimes be enough to debug from, but it's hopefully accompanied by a failure in an associated unit test that points more directly to the problem.

Breadth

Functional tests cover large parts of an application. For extremely small applications, it might be possible to write one single monolithic functional test that exercises the entire user experience.

Breadth is a dirty word when it comes to unit tests. If a unit test feels like it's covering any more that a few single points of possible failure, look for ways to break it out into multiple tests.

The project – jmad.us

Throughout this book we'll be building a real-life web application—the Jazz Musicianship Archive & Database, available at `http://jmad.us`. Improvisation is a tenant of jazz performance. JMAD is a tool for students of jazz to find particular solos by artist, instrument, key, or any number of other characteristics.

There are a number of user stories and acceptance criteria that we will implement throughout the book. We'll be focusing on the first and most simple one in this chapter:

[**As a Student, I want to search for Solos by basic attributes so that I can get better at improvisation.**]

Pretty straightforward, right? We've got a good noun "Solo" that will probably become a model, and a verb "search" that we can turn into a view. Let's get a little bit more specific with some acceptance criteria:

- Students can search by instrument, and/or artist
- Students can view search results
- Students can view a single solo detail page (including album, artist, and time info)

You probably already have some idea of how you'd like to build this out, so let's start the Django project.

Setting up your environment

There are a few prerequisites to get out of the way before we actually start on the project:

- You'll need Python installed on your computer. The project in this book is written with Python 3.4, but 2.7 or a later version will work just fine. Many OSs come with a version installed, but if you don't have it (or have an older version but want to use Python 3.4), look for instructions at `https://docs.python.org/3.4/using/`. I use Mac OSX and I prefer installing Python with Homebrew (`http://brew.sh/`).

- You should use a virtual environment for this project. Once you've got a version of Python installed, checkout out `virtualenv` (`http://docs.python-guide.org/en/latest/dev/virtualenvs/`) or `virtualenvwrapper` (`https://virtualenvwrapper.readthedocs.org/en/latest/`). These will allow you to keep separate installations of Python with their own installed packages. You'll need to activate that virtual environment each time you restart your terminal.

- Use `pip` to install packages in your environment. Once you get a virtual environment set up and activated, `pip` will be available in that environment.

This can be a bit of a pain to get going; some OSs are easier than others. Google is your friend, as am I. Tutorials abound on the internet, but email me at `hello@ kevinharvey.net` if you're really stuck.

Starting the project

Once you've got a Python environment set up, the next step is to create and move into a directory to start your project:

```
$ mkdir jmad-project
$ cd jmad-project
```

Now install Django and start a project called `jmad`:

```
$ pip install django
Downloading/unpacking django
   Downloading Django-1.8.1-py2.py3-none-any.whl (6.2MB): 6.2MB
downloaded
Installing collected packages: django
Successfully installed django
Cleaning up...
$ django-admin.py startproject jmad
```

To make sure we have got everything set up correctly, let's move into the project folder and try running tests:

```
$ cd jmad
$ python manage.py test
Creating test database for alias 'default'...


----------------------------------------------------------------------
Ran 0 tests in 0.000s


OK
Destroying test database for alias 'default'...
$
```

Believe it or not, this actually tells us something. We know that we've got a Django project where we can write some tests. We also know that our development environment is set up correctly since we didn't get any errors trying to run that command.

We've made some good progress, so let's set up our version control repository and make a commit. You'll need to install Git. Check out `http://git-scm.com/` for a version for your OS. Again, I'm on Mac so I use Homebrew.

Once you've got Git installed, initialize your project directory (one directory up from where you are now if you're following along) and run the following:

```
$ cd .. # takes us back to jmad-project
$ git init
```

You may want to add a remote to push your code to (GitHub is an excellent choice for this if you don't mind your code being open). Git has a ton of cool features that warrant their own book, we'll only scratch the surface.

Getting the sample code

All of the source code for this book is available at `https://github.com/kevinharvey/jmad`. I'll tag each commit in the book, and if you add my repository as a remote you'll be able to check out the code at the exact point you're at in the book (or you can just take a peek in your browser).

Here are the commands to add the new files and make the commit:

```
$ git add jmad
$ git commit -am 'initial project structure'
$ git tag -a ch2-1-init-project
```

To check out the repo at this commit, do `git checkout <tagname>`. In this instance, the command would be:

```
$ git checkout ch2-1-init-project
```

Starting a functional test

Our functional test will be the most direct link between the user stories and the application code. Let's start by fleshing out that user story into a narrative that we can follow. Add a `tests.py` file to the `jmad` app (one directory down from the project root) that Django created for us. We're going to need two imports to get us started, one of which will be a third-party package.

Introducing LiveServerTestCase

If you've done any testing at all with Python or Django, you've probably run into `TestCase`. The granddaddy class is from Python's `unittest`, and Django has a subclassed version of it that we'll use when we start writing unit tests. `LiveServerTestCase` is a further subclass, which provides not only the assertions that we'll need, but also starts a development server (similar to `python manage.py runserver`) that we can use to open the project in a browser during the test. Add the following to `jmad/jmad/tests.py`:

```
from django.test import LiveServerTestCase
```

So what good is having a development server running? Who is going to be opening a browser during our automated tests? Enter Selenium.

Introducing Selenium

Selenium is a tool for automating activity in a browser. You can use it to open new windows, visit web pages, click links, scroll around, and perform a number of other activities that a real user might in a browser. The bindings are available in the Python package of the same name:

```
$ pip install selenium
```

We're going to use the Selenium's Firefox WebDriver (the default and simplest to implement) to get started. If you don't already have Firefox installed on your system, you'll need a copy (`https://www.mozilla.org/en-US/firefox`).

Add the following import to `tests.py`:

```
from selenium import webdriver
```

With `LiveServerTestCase` and `selenium` imported, we can write this stub for our functional test:

```
class StudentTestCase(LiveServerTestCase):

    def setUp(self):
        self.browser = webdriver.Firefox()
        self.browser.implicitly_wait(2)
```

Here we're subclassing `LiveServerTestCase` to create our own test case, `StudentTestCase`, and setting up the web driver in `setUp()`.

The setUp() function is a method from the TestCase superclass that runs before each test method. We're setting up a new WebDriver instance (and therefore a fresh browser window) for each test. We're also using the web driver's implicitly_ wait() function to tell it to keep trying for at least two seconds before giving up on finding an element in the page.

Fleshing out the user story

Now that we've laid the groundwork, let's turn our user story into a real narrative. Start by creating another method for the test and writing out some user actions in comments:

```
    ...
    def test_student_find_solos(self):
        """
        Test that a user can search for solos
        """
        # Steve is a jazz student who would like to find more
        # examples of solos so he can improve his own
        # improvisation. He visits the home page of JMAD.

        # He knows he's in the right place because he can see
        # the name of the site in the heading.

        # He sees the inputs of the search form, including
        # labels and placeholders.

        # He types in the name of his instrument and submits
        # it.

        # He sees too many search results...

        # ...so he adds an artist to his search query and
        # gets a more manageable list.

        # He clicks on a search result.

        # The solo page has the title, artist and album for
        # this particular solo.

        # He also sees the start time and end time of the
        # solo.
```

The first item of note is the name of the test method. Any method on a `TestCase` subclass that starts with the `test_` prefix will run anytime we run `python manage.py test` (assuming that we haven't added an argument to exclude it). Test methods are typically named as a terse version of what the test actually tests.

Secondly, try to be descriptive about what the test is exercising in the docstring of the method (here we've added `Test that a user can search for solos`). The docstring is your chance to be a little verbose about what this test is doing.

Finally, the comments inside the method are spaced where we'll probably want to perform a user action, or test the state of the browser.

Getting the test to fail

We're going to be working through this functional test a little at a time, so we need a way to keep our place. Add the following line at the top of `test_student_find_solos`:

```
...
"""
self.fail('Incomplete Test')
...
```

Now move back to the top `jmad` directory and try running the test:

```
$ cd jmad
$ python manage.py test
Creating test database for alias 'default'...
F
======================================================================
FAIL: test_student_find_solos (jmad.tests.StudentTestCase)
----------------------------------------------------------------------
Traceback (most recent call last):
  File "/Users/kevin/dev/jmad-project/jmad/jmad/tests.py", line 16, in
test_student_find_solos
    self.fail('Incomplete Test')
AssertionError: Incomplete Test


----------------------------------------------------------------------
```

```
Ran 1 test in 2.512s
```

```
FAILED (failures=1)
```
```
Destroying test database for alias 'default'...
```
```
$
```

`self.fail` method simply forces the test to fail. Here we're using it to remind ourselves that we've still got work to do before this test is complete.

You should have a blank Firefox window on your screen right now. Selenium opened it in preparation for more commands (which we neglected to provide), and left it open because we never wrote the code to close it.

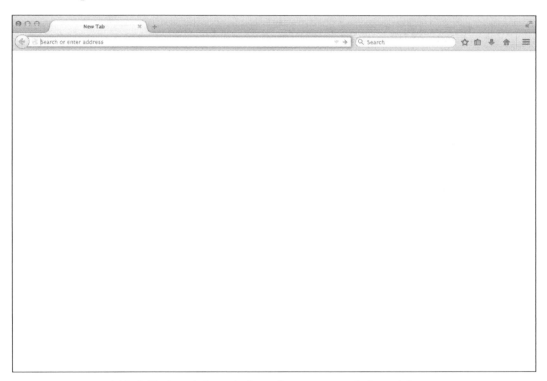

A blank Firefox window, similar to the one on your desktop right now

Let's fix that now. Add the following method below `setUp` in our test case:

```
    ...
    def tearDown(self):
        self.browser.quit()
```

Similar to `setUp`, `tearDown` runs after each test method. We can add any clean-up code we might need here, such as getting rid of open browser windows.

Run `python manage.py test` again. Notice how the FireFox window appears for only an instant and then disappears. Much nicer.

Opening a page with WebDriver

Looking back at our fleshed-out user story, the first action that's mentioned is something about visiting the home page. Let's extend our test to do that. Move the `self.fail()` line below the first comment block, and add a Selenium command:

```
...
# the home page of JMAD.
home_page = self.browser.get(self.live_server_url + '/')
self.fail('Incomplete Test')
...
```

Just as a browser sends a GET request to a server for a URL, we tell the `WebDriver` class to `get` a particular URL so that we can test it. In this case, we're asking for the home page. `self.live_server` evaluates to `http://localhost:8081` by default, and we append the trailing slash for good measure. We set the result of `get` to a variable called `home_page`, which we can test against and use to further navigate through the app.

Run the tests again (`python manage.py test`). You'll notice that not much has changed; it's still telling us that our test is incomplete. But in the flash of the browser opening and closing you might catch a glimpse of a 404 error as it tries to access a URL that we haven't defined in our application.

Finding elements with WebDriver

Finally, let's write some real test code. The next comment block in our functional test mentions seeing the name of the site in the heading. We'll need to look for it inside the page that we've saved in `home_page`. We can do that with Selenium's `find_element_by_css_selector` method.

It will be easier to use `find_element_by_css_selector` if we've got class and ID attributes. Let's plan to use Twitter Bootstrap to build out the front end of the site. That means we'll need the name of the site to be in an `<a>` tag with a class of `navbar-brand`. Add the following lines below the second comment block, and move the placeholder below it:

```
...
# of the site in the heading.
```

```
    brand_element = self.browser/
        .find_element_by_css_selector('.navbar-brand')
    self.assertEqual('JMAD', brand_element.text)
    self.fail('Incomplete Test')
    ...
```

Run the tests and you'll see the same Firefox flash and then what can only be described as a big mess in the terminal window. Here's the whole unfortunate traceback:

```
$ python manage.py test
Creating test database for alias 'default'...
E
======================================================================
ERROR: test_student_find_solos (jmad.tests.StudentTestCase)
----------------------------------------------------------------------
Traceback (most recent call last):
  File "/Users/kevin/dev/jmad-project/jmad/jmad/tests.py", line 25,
in test_student_find_solos
    brand_element = self.browser.find_element_by_css_selector('.navbar-
brand')
  File "/Users/kevin/.virtualenvs/jmad/lib/python3.4/site-
packages/selenium/webdriver/remote/webdriver.py", line 374, in
find_element_by_css_selector
    return self.find_element(by=By.CSS_SELECTOR, value=css_selector)
  File "/Users/kevin/.virtualenvs/jmad/lib/python3.4/site-
packages/selenium/webdriver/remote/webdriver.py", line 662, in
find_element
    {'using': by, 'value': value})['value']
  File "/Users/kevin/.virtualenvs/jmad/lib/python3.4/site-
packages/selenium/webdriver/remote/webdriver.py", line 173, in
execute
    self.error_handler.check_response(response)
  File "/Users/kevin/.virtualenvs/jmad/lib/python3.4/site-
packages/selenium/webdriver/remote/errorhandler.py", line 166, in
check_response
    raise exception_class(message, screen, stacktrace)
selenium.common.exceptions.NoSuchElementException: Message: Unable to
locate element: {"method":"css selector","selector":".navbar-brand"}
Stacktrace:
```

```
    at FirefoxDriver.prototype.findElementInternal_
(file:///var/folders/66/drtf6fkn183cszg_91f14mt00000gn/T/tmp6ya5p71x/
extensions/fxdriver@googlecode.com/components/driver-
component.js:9641:26)

    at fxdriver.Timer.prototype.setTimeout/<.notify
(file:///var/folders/66/drtf6fkn183cszg_91f14mt00000gn/T/tmp6ya5p71x/
extensions/fxdriver@googlecode.com/components/driver-
component.js:548:5)


----------------------------------------------------------------

Ran 1 test in 4.299s


FAILED (errors=1)

Destroying test database for alias 'default'...

$
```

```
● ○ ○                      jmad — bash — 86×28
ERROR: test_student_find_solos (jmad.tests.StudentTestCase)
-----------------------------------------------------------------------
Traceback (most recent call last):
  File "/Users/kevin/dev/jmad-project/jmad/jmad/tests.py", line 30, in test_student_fi
nd_solos
    brand_element = self.browser.find_element_by_css_selector('.navbar-brand')
  File "/Users/kevin/.virtualenvs/jmad/lib/python3.4/site-packages/selenium/webdriver/
remote/webdriver.py", line 376, in find_element_by_css_selector
    return self.find_element(by=By.CSS_SELECTOR, value=css_selector)
  File "/Users/kevin/.virtualenvs/jmad/lib/python3.4/site-packages/selenium/webdriver/
remote/webdriver.py", line 664, in find_element
    {'using': by, 'value': value})['value']
  File "/Users/kevin/.virtualenvs/jmad/lib/python3.4/site-packages/selenium/webdriver/
remote/webdriver.py", line 175, in execute
    self.error_handler.check_response(response)
  File "/Users/kevin/.virtualenvs/jmad/lib/python3.4/site-packages/selenium/webdriver/
remote/errorhandler.py", line 166, in check_response
    raise exception_class(message, screen, stacktrace)
selenium.common.exceptions.NoSuchElementException: Message: Unable to locate element:
{"method":"css selector","selector":".navbar-brand"}
Stacktrace:
    at FirefoxDriver.prototype.findElementInternal_ (file:///var/folders/66/drtf6fkn18
3cszg_91f14mt00000gn/T/tmp06fugsjx/extensions/fxdriver@googlecode.com/components/drive
r-component.js:10271)
    at fxdriver.Timer.prototype.setTimeout/<.notify (file:///var/folders/66/drtf6fkn18
3cszg_91f14mt00000gn/T/tmp06fugsjx/extensions/fxdriver@googlecode.com/components/drive
r-component.js:603)
```

Tracebacks involving Selenium can get ugly

See that line that starts with `selenium.common.exceptions.`
`NoSuchElementException`? What Selenium is trying to tell you here is that it wasn't
able to find an element by the selector `'.navbar-brand'`. That makes sense, since
we haven't added it to the application yet. Unfortunately the output of the test run at
this stage is hard to read and looks like something has gone seriously wrong.

In my book (and this is my book), this counts as progress: we've got a test that's failing that we need to get to pass. I'm making a commit.

```
$ git commit -am 'initial functional test scaffolding'
$ git tag -a ch2-2-init-func-test
```

Reading test output

Interpreting the often arcane output of the test runner is a key skill you'll pick up. Though at first it's frustrating, there will come a time when you have to track down a bug with only gobbledygook logs to wade through. The extra time you'll spend running TDD in the terminal will make the process much easier.

From here on out, I'm going to reduce the amount of test output I share in this book. If you're running the commands in the terminal you'll see much more. The most important parts will be printed here, so be sure to look for them in your own system.

Setting up a Django app for unit tests

We've gone as far as we can with the functional test as is, and we're ready to add some real functionality to the application. Let's start by adding an app to the project:

```
$ python manage.py startapp solos
```

Apps are often named for the main model that they contain. This app will contain the logic for managing and finding solos in our application. With the new app in place, here's what our directory structure now looks like:

```
jmad-project
- jmad
  - jmad
    - __init__.py
    - settings.py
    - tests.py
    - urls.py
    - wsgi.py
  - solos
    - migrations
      - __init__.py
    - __init__.py
    - admin.py
    - models.py
    - tests.py
    - views.py
  - manage.py
```

Django tips its cap to best practices by creating a `tests.py` file for us. Since we'll be writing lots of tests, let's convert it to a package to better organize our code. Here's the resulting `solos` app:

```
- solos
   - migrations
      - __init__.py
   - tests
      - __init__.py
   - __init__.py
   - admin.py
   - models.py
   - views.py
```

Finally, don't forget to add the `solos` app to `INSTALLED_APPS` in `jmad/settings.py`:

```
...
INSTALLED_APPS = (
    'django.contrib.admin',
    'django.contrib.auth',
    'django.contrib.contenttypes',
    'django.contrib.sessions',
    'django.contrib.messages',
    'django.contrib.staticfiles',
    'solos',
)
...
```

Planning our unit tests

This is probably a good time to stop and think about what our web application will actually be capable of doing. We're writing a piece of software that can:

- Accept HTTP requests at certain URLs
- Route those to the appropriate functions
- Access system resources as necessary to fulfill the logic in those functions
- Return a valid HTTP response

Let's start with the URL, which is the first part of our system that a user will encounter. Add a `test_urls.py` file to our new `solos.tests` package, and add the following code:

```
from django.test import TestCase
from django.core.urlresolvers import resolve

from solos.views import index

class SolosURLsTestCase(TestCase):

    def test_root_url_uses_index_view(self):
        """
        Test that the root of the site resolves to the
        correct view function
        """
        root = resolve('/')
        self.assertEqual(root.func, index)
```

At first blush, you'd be forgiven for thinking that this is overkill. As we'll see, this entire file only exists to test what will be one line of `urls.py` configuration (not counting imports). However, think about what this function does over the lifetime of our application. Forever after, we'll have a command that we can run to ensure that the root of our site routes to the right function. We're training our robot QA department to clean up after us when we build more of the site.

Now, run the tests:

```
$ python manage.py test
Creating test database for alias 'default'...
EE
...
======================================================================
ERROR: solos.tests.test_views (unittest.loader.ModuleImportFailure)
----------------------------------------------------------------------
...
ImportError: cannot import name 'index'
...
```

Points for you if you saw that coming—we tried to import something that didn't exist yet.

Finally writing application code

Okay, we're finally at a place where we can write some of the application! Let's open up `solos/views.py`, erase what's there, and stub out our `index` function:

```
...
def index():
    pass
```

I'm being deliberately Spartan here, almost blindly letting the output of the test drive the code I write. Let's run the tests again:

```
$ python manage.py test
Creating test database for alias 'default'...
EE
======================================================================
ERROR: test_root_url_uses_index_view (solos.tests.test_urls.
SoloViewTestCase)
----------------------------------------------------------------------
...
  File "/Users/kevin/.virtualenvs/jmad/lib/python3.4/site-
packages/django/core/urlresolvers.py", line 358, in resolve
    raise Resolver404({'tried': tried, 'path': new_path})
django.core.urlresolvers.Resolver404: {'tried': [[<RegexURLResolver
<RegexURLPattern list> (admin:admin) ^admin/>]], 'path': ''}
...
```

Django gave me a big fat 404 when it attempted to resolve that URL (`'/'`). We'll need to wire it up to our new `index` function in `urls.py`. Here's what `jmad/urls.py` should look like (including the `'admin/'` URL that was created when my project was initialized):

```
from django.conf.urls import include, url
from django.contrib import admin

urlpatterns = [
    url(r'^$', 'solos.views.index'),
    url(r'^admin/', include(admin.site.urls)),
]
```

Now, the tests:

```
$ python manage.py test
Creating test database for alias 'default'...
```

```
.E
========================================================================
ERROR: test_student_find_solos (jmad.tests.StudentTestCase)
------------------------------------------------------------------------

...
```

See the little dot before E? That's our first passing test! We have now locked down that the root of our site uses our `index` function. TDD is all about small, accumulated victories. Let's put our trophy in the case:

```
$ git add solos
$ git commit -am 'initial solos app, route to index view'
$ git tag -a ch2-3-init-solos-app
```

You may have noticed in our last test run that the error in the browser changed from a 'Not Found' to an 'Internal Server Error (500)'. This probably has something to do with our comically lightweight `index` function. Let's build that out further with a test.

Testing views with RequestFactory

`RequestFactory` is a tool for creating and fine-tuning HTTP requests that we can use to test view functions. You can think of it as a stripped-down version of Selenium's WebDriver.

Add a new file `test_views.py` to `solos/test` with the following code:

```python
from django.test import TestCase, RequestFactory

from solos.views import index

class IndexViewTestCase(TestCase):

    def setUp(self):
        self.factory = RequestFactory()

    def test_index_view_basic(self):
        """
        Test that index view returns a 200 response and uses
        the correct template
        """
        request = self.factory.get('/')
        response = index(request)
        self.assertEqual(response.status_code, 200)
```

Here we're using the simplest possible implementation of `RequestFactory`, creating a new GET request and providing it as the first argument to the `index` function that we wrote earlier. Let's run the tests:

```
$ python manage.py test
Creating test database for alias 'default'...
.EE
======================================================================
ERROR: test_index_view_basic (solos.tests.test_views.IndexViewTestCase)
----------------------------------------------------------------------
Traceback (most recent call last):
  File "/Users/kevin/dev/jmad-project/jmad/solos/tests/test_views.py",
line 16, in test_index_view_basic
    response = index(request)
TypeError: index() takes 0 positional arguments but 1 was given
...
```

Oh yeah, we didn't write `index` to take any arguments. We're continuing the omniscient test programmer/ignorant application programmer theme here for a couple of reasons. First, we're trying to guard against writing any more than the necessary code to get the job done. This ideal is typically referred to as YAGNI, which stands for "You ain't gonna need it." Any code written *in anticipation* of needing it runs the danger of adding unnecessary work. Secondly, it's an attempt to show tiny steps being taken in TDD. As you get more comfortable with the methodology, you may decide to bite off a bit more functionality at the first go (in a similar way to starting view functions with the right arguments).

Let's take care of this latest error by updating our index function to accept an argument:

```
...
def index(request):
    pass
```

Now how does it look?

```
$ python manage.py test
Creating test database for alias 'default'...
.EE
======================================================================
ERROR: test_index_view_basic (solos.tests.test_views.IndexViewTestCase)
----------------------------------------------------------------------
```

```
Traceback (most recent call last):
  File "/Users/kevin/dev/jmad-project/jmad/solos/tests/test_views.py",
line 17, in test_index_view_basic
    self.assertEqual(response.status_code, 200)
AttributeError: 'NoneType' object has no attribute 'status_code'
...
```

Looking at the error message, our test runner is looking for an attribute called `status_code` on a variable that is evaluating to `None`. One line up in the traceback, we can see that variable is the response. As you probably noticed, we didn't return a value from `index()`. Let's fix that now:

```
from django.http import HttpResponse


def index(request):
    return HttpResponse()
```

And test it, as follows:

```
$ python manage.py test
Creating test database for alias 'default'...
..E
======================================================================
ERROR: test_student_find_solos (jmad.tests.StudentTestCase)
----------------------------------------------------------------------
...
File "/Users/kevin/.virtualenvs/jmad/lib/python3.4/site-packages/
selenium/webdriver/remote/errorhandler.py", line 166, in check_response
    raise exception_class(message, screen, stacktrace)
selenium.common.exceptions.NoSuchElementException: Message: Unable to
locate element: {"method":"css selector","selector":".navbar-brand"}
Stacktrace:
...
```

Cool, our unit test passes in its current form, but we're still not any further on our functional test. We need a template. Let's extend our current unit test to check that our response from our view uses a template. Update `solos/tests/test_views.py` as follows:

```
        ...
        request = self.factory.get('/')
        with self.assertTemplateUsed('solos/index.html'):
```

```
                    response = index(request)
                    self.assertEqual(response.status_code, 200)
```

The `with` clause in the preceding code snippet is how we use `assertTemplateUsed()` as a context manager. There are a number of assertions that are used in this way. Here we're testing that a template called `'solos/index.html'` is used when that response is rendered. Here's the failing test:

```
$ python manage.py test
Creating test database for alias 'default'...
.FE
...
======================================================================
FAIL: test_index_view_basic (solos.tests.test_views.IndexViewTestCase)
----------------------------------------------------------------------
Traceback (most recent call last):
  File "/Users/kevin/dev/jmad-project/jmad/solos/tests/test_views.py",
line 18, in test_index_view_basic
    self.assertEqual(response.status_code, 200)
  File "/Users/kevin/.virtualenvs/jmad/lib/python3.4/site-packages/
django/test/testcases.py", line 151, in __exit__
    self.test_case.fail(message)
AssertionError: solos/index.html was not rendered. No template was
rendered.
...
```

We get a refreshingly clear error message here: no template got rendered in the code block inside that context manager. We need to make a couple of changes to get this to pass. First, let's update our `index` view to render a template for the response that it returns:

```
    from django.shortcuts import render_to_response


    def index(request):
        return render_to_response('solos/index.html')
```

Now we need to create a template. Create the `solos/templates/solos/index.html` file and directories, leaving it empty for now, and run the tests again:

```
$ python manage.py test
Creating test database for alias 'default'...
..E
```

```
=======================================================================
ERROR: test_student_find_solos (jmad.tests.StudentTestCase)
-----------------------------------------------------------------------
...

File "/Users/kevin/.virtualenvs/jmad/lib/python3.4/site-packages/
selenium/webdriver/remote/errorhandler.py", line 166, in check_response
    raise exception_class(message, screen, stacktrace)
selenium.common.exceptions.NoSuchElementException: Message: Unable to
locate element: {"method":"css selector","selector":".navbar-brand"}
...

-----------------------------------------------------------------------
Ran 3 tests in 4.187s


FAILED (errors=1)
Destroying test database for alias 'default'...
```

We're back where we started, with our unit tests passing and our incomplete functional test failing. This is progress, and we commit progress:

```
$ git add solos/tests
$ git commit -am 'initial index template, view test'
$ git tag -a ch2-4-init-index-template
```

Now that we have a template being rendered, we can actually write the code to move forward with the functional test. Since I know we'll be using Bootstrap, but I don't know anything else about the implementation, I'm only going to add the necessary HTML to the template to make my test happy:

```
<a class="navbar-brand">JMAD</a>
```

Run the tests:

```
$ python manage.py test
Creating test database for alias 'default'...
..F
=======================================================================
FAIL: test_student_find_solos (jmad.tests.StudentTestCase)
-----------------------------------------------------------------------
...

AssertionError: Incomplete Test
...
```

Excellent! We're back at our placeholder in the functional test. Let's commit once more:

```
$ git commit -am 'Adds heading to index.html'
$ git tag -a ch2-5-adds-index-heading
```

Continuing through the functional test

Let's keep going, shall we? Move the placeholder down and add the following below the next comment block:

```
# He sees the inputs of the search form, including labels and
# placeholders.
instrument_input = self.browser.find_element_by_css_selector(
    'input#jmad-instrument'
)
self.assertIsNotNone(self.browser.find_element_by_css_selector(
        'label[for="jmad-instrument"]'))
self.assertEqual(instrument_input.get_attribute('placeholder'),
    'i.e. trumpet')
artist_input = self.browser.find_element_by_css_selector(
    'input#jmad-artist')
self.assertIsNotNone(self.browser.find_element_by_css_selector(
    'label[for="jmad-artist"]'))
self.assertEqual(artist_input.get_attribute('placeholder'),
    'i.e. Davis')


self.fail('Incomplete Test')
```

We're going to look for an input and confirm that its placeholder attribute gives us some helpful information. You know the drill by now:

```
$ python manage.py test
Creating test database for alias 'default'...
..E
======================================================================
ERROR: test_student_find_solos (jmad.tests.StudentTestCase)
----------------------------------------------------------------------
...
```

```
      raise exception_class(message, screen, stacktrace)
selenium.common.exceptions.NoSuchElementException: Message: Unable to
locate element: {"method":"css selector","selector":"input#jmad-
instrument"}

...
```

Here's more hard-to-read test output. Once again, it's telling us that it couldn't find the element that it's looking for, as expected. Let's add the instrument and artist fields to `solos/templates/solos/index.html`. The entire file should now be:

```
<a class="navbar-brand">JMAD</a>

    <label for="jmad-instrument">Instrument</label>
    <input type="text" class="form-control" id="jmad-instrument"
          name="instrument" placeholder="i.e. trumpet" />
    <label for="jmad-artist">Artist</label>
    <input type="text" class="form-control" id="jmad-artist"
          name="artist" placeholder="i.e. Davis" />
```

Now, run the tests:

```
$ python manage.py test
Creating test database for alias 'default'...
..F
======================================================================
FAIL: test_student_find_solos (jmad.tests.StudentTestCase)
----------------------------------------------------------------------
...
AssertionError: Incomplete Test
...
```

And on to the next comment. Update the test with the following code, moving the placeholder down as we go:

```
    ...
    # He types in the name of his instrument and clicks the submit button
    instrument_input.send_keys('saxophone')
    instrument_input.submit()
    self.fail('Incomplete Test')
```

`send_keys` lets us type in an input element, and `submit` allows us to submit a form. Run the following tests:

```
$ python manage.py test
Creating test database for alias 'default'...
..E
======================================================================
ERROR: test_student_find_solos (jmad.tests.StudentTestCase)
----------------------------------------------------------------------
...

selenium.common.exceptions.NoSuchElementException: Message: Element was
not in a form so couldn't submit
```

Another ugly traceback, but here's a new message that tells us exactly what to do next. We tried to submit an input element, but we got `Element was not in a form so couldn't submit`. Let's wrap it, and while we're at it add a button to click:

```
    ...
    <form>
        <label for="jmad-instrument">Instrument</label>
        <input type="text" class="form-control" id="jmad-instrument"
            name="instrument" placeholder="i.e. trumpet" />
        <label for="jmad-artist">Artist</label>
        <input type="text" class="form-control" id="jmad-artist"
            name="artist" placeholder="i.e. Davis" />

        <button type="submit">Search JMAD</button>
    </form>
```

Now update the test to use the new button:

```
    ...
    instrument_input.send_keys('saxophone')
    self.browser\
        .find_element_by_css_selector('form button').click()
```

You can download the example code files from your account at `http://www. packtpub.com` for all the Packt Publishing books you have purchased. If you purchased this book elsewhere, you can visit `http://www.packtpub.com/support` and register to have the files e-mailed directly to you.

The source code for the sample application is also available on GitHub at `https://github.com/kevinharvey/jmad` on the `test-driven-django-development` branch (the repository's default). Development milestones in the book have been tagged with names like `ch5-2-staff-login` to make navigating the repository easier.

Run the tests and you'll see we're back to our placeholder. Nice! Also, here's what you'd see in Firefox if you halted the script before the failure:

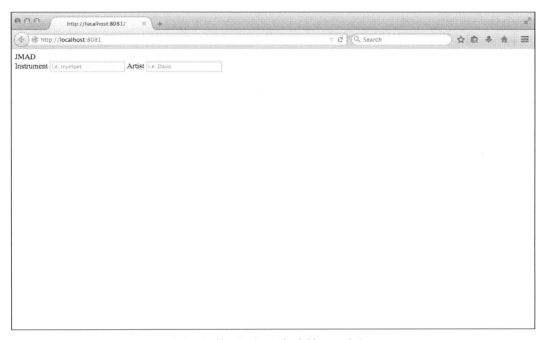

It's actually starting to look like a website

On to the next comment block:

```
...
# He sees too many search results, so he adds a particular
# artist to his search query
search_results = self.browser.find_elements_by_css_selector(
    '.jmad-search-result'
)
self.assertGreater(len(search_results), 2)
self.fail('Incomplete Test')
...
```

Wow, our test user is awfully impatient wading through search results. You may have missed it, but we're using a different selector here, `find_elements_by_css_selector()` (notice the additional `s` in `elements`) returns a list of any elements that match the CSS selector. Here, we're trying to find some elements that we will identify by namespaced classes. Let's trick this test into passing. Update the template with the following:

```
...
</form>

<div class="jmad-search-result"></div>
<div class="jmad-search-result"></div>
<div class="jmad-search-result"></div>
```

Run the tests, and we hit the placeholder. It may seem like we're cheating, but all's fair as long as we're not done with the test. Let's move on.

Here's some more functional test code, including a rephrased comment that flows better with our WebDriver script:

```
...
# ... so he adds a particular artist to his search query and
# gets a more manageable list
second_artist_input = self.browser\
    .find_element_by_css_selector('input#jmad-artist')
second_artist_input.send_keys('Cannonball Adderley')
self.browser\
    .find_element_by_css_selector('form button').click()
second_search_results = self.browser\
    .find_elements_by_css_selector('.jmad-search-result')
self.assertEqual(len(second_search_results), 2)
self.fail('Incomplete Test')
```

And the result of the test run:

```
$ python manage.py test
Creating test database for alias 'default'...
..F
======================================================================
FAIL: test_student_find_solos (jmad.tests.StudentTestCase)
----------------------------------------------------------------------
Traceback (most recent call last):
  File "/Users/kevin/dev/jmad-project/jmad/jmad/tests.py", line 46, in
test_student_find_solos
```

```
    self.assertEqual(len(second_search_results), 2)
AssertionError: 3 != 2

...
```

Thanks to our growing test coverage, our cheap `jmad-search-result` trick did not pan out. We know our application needs to return dynamic results based on user input, so we can't just change the test to expect three results again. It's time to get our search form working. But first, a commit:

```
$ git commit -am 'Adds form elements, fake search results to
index.html.'

$ git tag -a ch2-6-adds-form-elements
```

Adding search to the view

Let's stop for another minute and assess what we're trying to accomplish. In the latest version of our test, we send a couple of form inputs and receive differing numbers of search results. Sounds like we'll need to:

1. Handle search terms in our view

2. Create a model to store some data

3. Return some of that data in our view based on the search term

4. Render that data in our template

Let's add a new test to `solos/tests/test_views.py` to make sure that we can handle search terms via GET parameters. Update `IndexViewTestCase` with the following code:

```
from django.test import TestCase, RequestFactory
from django.db.models.query import QuerySet

...

class IndexViewTestCase(TestCase):
    def setUp(self):
        self.factory = RequestFactory()

...

    def test_index_view_returns_solos(self):
        """
        Test that the index view will attempt to return
        Solos if query parameters exist
        """
```

```
                        response = self.client.get(
                            '/',
                            {'instrument': 'drums'}
                        )
                        self.assertIs(
                            type(response.context['solos']),
                            QuerySet
                        )
```

Say hello to Django's test client (referenced here as `self.client`), a sort of dummy browser that can send requests to URLs. We're using it instead of `RequestFactory`, so that we'll have access to the `response.context` dictionary, to make sure that our view is building the correct response.

We sent in a GET parameter with the request, and we test that the response has a `QuerySet` called `'solos'` in its context. Note that the `QuerySet` may be empty, and this test will still pass. Run the tests:

```
$ python manage.py test
Creating test database for alias 'default'...
..EF
======================================================================
ERROR: test_index_view_returns_solos (solos.tests.test_views.
IndexViewTestCase)
----------------------------------------------------------------------
...
KeyError: 'solos'
...
```

Right, let's add `solos` to the response:

```
    def index(request):
        context = {'solos': None}
        return render_to_response('solos/index.html', context)
```

Run the tests again:

```
$ python manage.py test
Creating test database for alias 'default'...
..FF
======================================================================
```

```
FAIL: test_index_view_returns_solos (solos.tests.test_views.
IndexViewTestCase)
-----------------------------------------------------------------
Traceback (most recent call last):
  File "/Users/kevin/dev/jmad-project/jmad/solos/tests/test_views.py",
line 27, in test_index_view_returns_solos
    self.assertIs(type(response.context['solos']), QuerySet)
AssertionError: <class 'NoneType'> is not <class 'django.db.models.query.
QuerySet'>
...
```

Yep, it's not a `QuerySet`. Let's make it one:

```
    ...
    context = {'solos': Solo.objects.all()}
    ...
```

What did that do for us?

```
$ python manage.py test
Creating test database for alias 'default'...
.EEE
=================================================================
ERROR: test_index_view_basic (solos.tests.test_views.IndexViewTestCase)
-----------------------------------------------------------------
...
NameError: name 'Solo' is not defined


=================================================================
ERROR: test_index_view_returns_solos (solos.tests.test_views.
IndexViewTestCase)
-----------------------------------------------------------------
...
NameError: name 'Solo' is not defined
```

Okay, I can define `Solo`:

```
    ...
    from .models import Solo
    ...
```

Now?

```
$ python manage.py test
Creating test database for alias 'default'...
EEE
...
=======================================================================
ERROR: solos.tests.test_urls (unittest.loader.ModuleImportFailure)
-----------------------------------------------------------------------
...
File "/Users/kevin/dev/jmad-project/jmad/solos/views.py", line 3, in
<module>
    from .models import Solo
ImportError: cannot import name 'Solo'
```

Not quite. We need to create our model. Let's leave this view test for a moment and go take care of our first model. Create a new file `solos/tests/test_models.py`. The following test will ensure that `Solo`'s API will be in place:

```python
from django.test import TestCase

from solos.models import Solo


class SoloModelTestCase(TestCase):

    def setUp(self):
        self.solo = Solo.objects.create(
            track='Falling in Love with Love',
            artist='Oscar Peterson',
            instrument='piano'
        )

    def test_solo_basic(self):
        """
        Test the basic functionality of Solo
        """
        self.assertEqual(self.solo.artist, 'Peterson')
```

If we ran the tests now, we'd see the same error that we've been seeing, except we'd be seeing it from a new test: `ImportError: cannot import name 'Solo'`. Let's get that fixed. Open `solos/models.py` and add the following:

```
Solo = None
```

That doesn't exactly get our test to pass, but it's all we need to get to the next failure message:

```
$ python manage.py test
Creating test database for alias 'default'...
E.EEE
======================================================================
ERROR: test_solo_basic (solos.tests.test_models.SoloModelTestCase)
----------------------------------------------------------------------
Traceback (most recent call last):
  File "/Users/kevin/dev/jmad-project/jmad/solos/tests/test_models.py",
line 9, in setUp
    self.solo = Solo.objects.create(
AttributeError: 'NoneType' object has no attribute 'objects'
...
```

`Solo` needs an `'objects'` attribute, which would come from its model manager, which it would have if it were a model. Update `solos/models.py` to look as follows:

```
from django.db import models

class Solo(models.Model):
    pass
```

This will look very familiar if you've done much work with Django. We're subclassing `Model` for our solo model, which will give it an `objects` attribute. Run some tests and we'll see a new error.

```
$ python manage.py test
...
sqlite3.OperationalError: no such table: solos_solo


The above exception was the direct cause of the following exception:


...

django.db.utils.OperationalError: no such table: solos_solo
```

What Django is trying to tell us with this database error is that there's no table for the solos, because we haven't created a migration for our `Solo` model yet.

You may have noticed that at no point in our development have we run `./manage.py migrate`, or even `./manage.py runserver`. We're letting the Django test runner build the database for us from scratch each time and delete it after we're done.

Go ahead and create your migration:

```
$ python manage.py makemigrations
Migrations for 'solos':
  0001_initial.py:
    - Create model Solo
```

Try the tests again:

```
$ python manage.py test
Creating test database for alias 'default'...
E...F
======================================================================
ERROR: test_solo_basic (solos.tests.test_models.SoloModelTestCase)
----------------------------------------------------------------------
...
TypeError: 'track' is an invalid keyword argument for this function


======================================================================
FAIL: test_student_find_solos (jmad.tests.StudentTestCase)
----------------------------------------------------------------------
...
AssertionError: 3 != 2
...
```

The test runner is trying to add a `'track'` to the solo via a keyword argument, but our model is not having it. Let's add some fields to the model:

```
class Solo(models.Model):
    track = models.CharField(max_length=100)
    artist = models.CharField(max_length=100)
    instrument = models.CharField(max_length=50)
```

And run the tests:

```
$ python manage.py test
...
sqlite3.OperationalError: no such column: solos_solo.track


The above exception was the direct cause of the following exception:
...
django.db.utils.OperationalError: no such column: solos_solo.track
```

The database doesn't have the right columns for our solo yet. No bother, just run `python manage.py makemigrations`, then test again. Django's migration tool will complain about non-nullable fields needing defaults. Choose option 1 throughout:

```
$ python manage.py makemigrations
You are trying to add a non-nullable field 'artist' to solo without a
default; we can't do that (the database needs something to populate
existing rows).
Please select a fix:
 1) Provide a one-off default now (will be set on all existing rows)
 2) Quit, and let me add a default in models.py
Select an option: 1
Please enter the default value now, as valid Python
The datetime and django.utils.timezone modules are available, so you
can do e.g. timezone.now()
>>> 'n/a'
...
[repeats twice more]
...
Migrations for 'solos':
  0002_auto_20141230_0800.py:
    - Add field artist to solo
    - Add field instrument to solo
    - Add field track to solo
```

And test again:

```
$ python manage.py test
Creating test database for alias 'default'...
....F
```

```
=======================================================================
FAIL: test_student_find_solos (jmad.tests.StudentTestCase)
-----------------------------------------------------------------------
...

AssertionError: 3 != 2
```

Four of five tests passed! That means we're getting a `QuerySet` in our context and we can create solos. Let's build out the view test a little to see it in action:

```python
...
from solos.models import Solo

class IndexViewTestCase(TestCase):

    def setUp(self):
        ...
        self.drum_solo = Solo.objects.create(
            instrument='drums',
            artist='Rich',
            track='Bugle Call Rag'
        )
        self.bass_solo = Solo.objects.create(
            instrument='saxophone',
            artist='Coltrane',
            track='Mr. PC'
        )

    def test_index_view_returns_solos(self):
        """
        Test that the index view will attempt to return Solos
        if query parameters exist
        """
        response = self.client.get(
            '/',
            {'instrument': 'drums'}
        )

        solos = response.context['solos']

        self.assertIs(type(solos), QuerySet)
        self.assertEqual(len(solos), 1)
        self.assertEqual(solos[0].artist, 'Rich')
```

We've created two solo objects in the `setUp` function, which we'll be able to use to test our view. We've also refactored a bit to set the `'solos'` `QuerySet` to a variable for reuse. Here are our tests now:

```
$ python manage.py test
Creating test database for alias 'default'...
...FF
======================================================================
FAIL: test_index_view_returns_solos (solos.tests.test_views.
IndexViewTestCase)
----------------------------------------------------------------------
Traceback (most recent call last):
  File "/Users/kevin/dev/jmad-project/jmad/solos/tests/test_views.py",
line 34, in test_index_view_returns_solos
    self.assertEqual(len(solos), 1)
AssertionError: 2 != 1

...
```

It would appear that our view is finding two solos when we only expected one. The culprit is the `all()` selector in our view. Let's update it to filter on instrument:

```
def index(request):
    context = {'solos': Solo.objects.filter(
        instrument=request.GET.get(
            'instrument', None
        )
    )}
    return render_to_response('solos/index.html', context)
```

If we run the tests, we'll see that `test_index_view_returns_solos` now passes. Let's take a moment to commit our work:

```
$ git add solos/migrations/
$ git commit -am 'Adds Solo model, implemented in index view'
$ git tag -a ch2-7-add-solo-model
```

We can now continue on the view and template to get the functional test past its current error. The functional test is looking for three saxophone solos, two of which should be by Cannonball Adderley. Let's add those to `setUp` in `jmad/tests.py`:

```
    from solos.models import Solo
    ...
    def setUp(self):
```

```
    ...
    self.solo1 = Solo.objects.create(
        instrument='saxophone',
        artist='John Coltrane',
        track='My Favorite Things'
    )
    self.solo2 = Solo.objects.create(
        instrument='saxophone',
        artist='Cannonball Adderley',
        track='All Blues'
    )
    self.solo3 = Solo.objects.create(
        instrument='saxophone',
        artist='Cannonball Adderley',
        track='Waltz for Debby'
    )
```

Now, let's update the template to use those new models. Update `solos/templates/solos/index.html`, replacing the three repeated `div`s with the following:

```
...
{% for solo in solos %}
    <div class="jmad-search-result">
        {{ solo.track }}: {{ solo.artist }} on
        {{ solo.instrument }}
    </div>
{% endfor %}
```

How do our tests look now?

```
$ python manage.py test
Creating test database for alias 'default'...
....F
======================================================================
FAIL: test_student_find_solos (jmad.tests.StudentTestCase)
----------------------------------------------------------------------
Traceback (most recent call last):
  File "/Users/kevin/dev/jmad-project/jmad/jmad/tests.py", line 57, in
test_student_find_solos
    self.assertEqual(len(second_search_results), 2)
AssertionError: 0 != 2

...
```

We've suffered a little bit of regression since we removed our three `div` hack. Let's work on the view to get this right. Back to `solos/views.py`:

```
...
def index(request):
    context = {'solos': []}

    if request.GET.keys():
        solos_queryset = Solo.objects.all()

        if request.GET.get('instrument', None):
            solos_queryset = solos_queryset.filter(
                instrument=request.GET.get(
                    'instrument',
                    None
                )
            )

        if request.GET.get('artist', None):
            solos_queryset = solos_queryset.filter(
                artist=request.GET.get('artist', None)
            )

        context['solos'] = solos_queryset

    return render_to_response('solos/index.html', context)
```

One more test run:

```
$ python manage.py test
Creating test database for alias 'default'...
....F
=====================================================================
FAIL: test_student_find_solos (jmad.tests.StudentTestCase)
---------------------------------------------------------------------
...
AssertionError: Incomplete Test
...
```

And we're back at our placeholder.

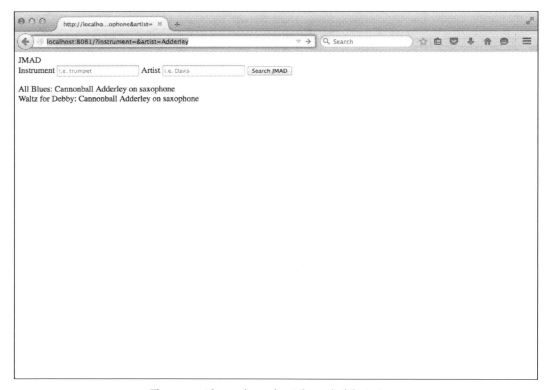

The page with search results at the end of the test run

Let's commit before we forge ahead:

```
$ git commit -am 'Adds filtering to index and model data to template'
$ git tag -a ch2-8-add-filtering
```

Summary

In this chapter, we gathered requirements for our sample project, set up our development environment, and started a Django project. We discussed the difference between functional tests and unit tests, and wrote a few unit tests for Django URLs, views, and models. We partially completed the first user story for our project using TDD, learning the basics of building browser-based tests with `LiveServerTestCase` and `Selenium`.

In the next chapter, we will dig deeper into `LiveServerTestCase` and `Selenium` as we continue to build out our sample project.

3
Ironclad Code

In this chapter, we're going to learn more about the tools available for unit testing in Django. In order to do that, we will:

- Pick up where we left off on the previous chapter's functional test
- Explore the assertions available to us in TestCase
- Compare ways to generate web requests in tests
- Refactor a bit

Though we'll be focusing on tools for writing unit tests in this chapter, we'll be doing so in the context of continuing to work through (and build out) our functional test. One of the greatest benefits of TDD is how easy it is to come back to your work after a break. Just run the tests again to see where we are:

```
$ python manage.py test
Creating test database for alias 'default'...
....F
======================================================================
FAIL: test_student_find_solos (jmad.tests.StudentTestCase)
----------------------------------------------------------------------
Traceback (most recent call last):
  File "/Users/kevin/dev/jmad-project/jmad/jmad/tests.py", line 57, in
test_student_find_solos
    self.fail('Incomplete Test')
AssertionError: Incomplete Test
```

```
------------------------------------------------------------------------

Ran 5 tests in 2.480s


FAILED (failures=1)
Destroying test database for alias 'default'...
```

At line 55 of `jmad/tests.py`, we find:

```
    ...

            second_search_results = self.browser\
                .find_elements_by_css_selector(
                    '.jmad-search-result a'
                )
            self.assertEqual(len(second_search_results), 2)
            self.fail('Incomplete Test')

            # He clicks on one of the search results.
    ...
```

Add the following lines after the comment and move the `self.fail` placeholder to the next line:

```
    ...

            self.assertEqual(len(second_search_results), 2)

            # He clicks on a search result.
              second_search_results[0].click()
            self.fail('Incomplete Test')
    ...
```

Run the tests once more and we'll make it to the placeholder. Our next comment hints at a new page and a few new fields for our model:

```
            # On the solo page he sees the title, artist and album for
            # this particular solo.

            # He also sees the start time and end time of the solo.
```

Complete the test as shown here. No need to move the placeholder, as this will exercise everything we need in the functional test for now:

```
            # On the solo page he sees the title, artist and album for
            # this particular solo.
            self.assertEqual(
```

```
        self.browser.current_url,
        '{}/solos/2/'.format(self.live_server_url)
)


    self.assertEqual(
        self.browser.find_element_by_css_selector(
            '#jmad-artist').text,
        'Cannonball Adderley'
)
self.assertEqual(
        self.browser.find_element_by_css_selector(
            '#jmad-track').text,
        'All Blues'
)
self.assertEqual(
        self.browser.find_element_by_css_selector(
            '#jmad-album').text,
        'Kind of Blue'
)


# He also sees the start time and end time of the solo.
self.assertEqual(
        self.browser.find_element_by_css_selector(
            '#jmad-start-time').text,
        '2:06'
)
self.assertEqual(
        self.browser.find_element_by_css_selector(
            '#jmad-end-time').text,
        '4:01'
)
```

Since we haven't done anything to make a solo page available, none of this works. Our test of the browser's `current_url` fails since we haven't left the home page. Before we figure out what's going on, let's commit:

```
$ git commit -am 'Finishes first iteration of functional test'
$ git tag -a ch3-1-finish-func-test
```

Using the Python Debugger in tests

Selenium blows through the test case faster than we can see the page in the browser. Since our test is just a Python script, we have access to my favorite debugging tool—pdb.

pdb, a.k.a. the Python Debugger, is a tremendously helpful utility in the standard library. It allows us, among other things, to break execution anywhere in our source code and have a peak around as if we were in a regular Python terminal, but with all the current variables defined. Check out the docs at `https://docs.python.org/3.4/library/pdb.html`.

Add the following lines just before the failing assertion:

```
# On the solo page he sees the title, artist and album for
# this particular solo.
import pdb;pdb.set_trace()
self.assertEqual(
    self.browser.current_url,
    '{}/solos/2/'.format(self.live_server_url)
)
```

`pdb.set_trace()` will halt the test, leaving Firefox open and waiting for our input in the terminal. When we run the test, we see that the browser has the list of solos that we specified. Selenium was able to `click()` the element, but of course nothing happens when you click on a `<div>`. We need to hyperlink those search results.

We'll explore more of the debugger's methods later, but for now we can type c to continue through the test. Don't forget to remove the debugger once the test is finished.

Using RequestFactory

Just as we used `RequestFactory` in the last chapter to test the index view, let's use it to write a test for the view that we need. Add the following new class to the bottom of `solos/tests/test_views.py`:

```
class SoloViewTestCase(TestCase):

    def setUp(self):
        self.factory = RequestFactory()

    def test_basic(self):
        """
```

```
Test that the solo view returns a 200 response, uses
the correct template, and has the correct context
"""
request = self.factory.get('/solos/1/')

response = SoloDetailView.as_view()(
    request,
    self.drum_solo.pk
)

self.assertEqual(response.status_code, 200)
  self.assertEqual(
      response.context_data['solo'].artist,
      'Rich'
  )
with self\
    .assertTemplateUsed('solos/solo_detail.html'):
      response.render()
```

This should look familiar, but with one important change. We're going to use a class-based view for the individual solo pages (hence the `as_view` method call). That, combined with our decision to use the `RequestFactory` for this test (as opposed to the `self.client`) means we'll have to call the `render` method on the response to check if it's using the right template.

Note that here we're testing the `context_data` dictionary on the response. This is where `DetailView` puts the single object for use in rendering the template. In this case, it's a `Solo`.

Running a single test with dot notation

So far, we've been running the entire test suite, but what if we want to run just a single test, or a portion of the tests? We can use standard dot notation to specify which tests to run, like so:

```
# Run all the tests in the solos app
$ python manage.py test solos


# Run all the tests in solos/tests/test_views.py
$ python manage.py test solos.tests.test_views
```

```
# Run all the tests in SoloViewTestCase
$ python manage.py test solos.tests.test_views.SoloViewTestCase


# Run only test_basic in SoloViewTestCase
$ python manage.py test solos.tests.test_views.SoloViewTestCase.\
test_basic
```

Let's try using dot notation to run SoloTestCase.test_basic. Our first run will go well, but we'll see a tricky gotcha in the second.

```
$ python manage.py test solos.tests.test_views.SoloViewTestCase.test_
basic
Creating test database for alias 'default'...
E
======================================================================
ERROR: test_basic (solos.tests.test_views.SoloViewTestCase)
----------------------------------------------------------------------
Traceback (most recent call last):
  File "/Users/kevin/dev/jmad-project/jmad/solos/tests/test_views.py",
line 50, in test_basic
    response = SoloDetailView.as_view()(request, self.drum_solo.pk)
NameError: name 'SoloDetailView' is not defined


----------------------------------------------------------------------
Ran 1 test in 0.001s


FAILED (errors=1)
Destroying test database for alias 'default'...
```

No problem, we can fix that easily. Just add the view to the import statement already at the top of the file:

```
from solos.views import index, SoloDetailView
...
```

Now run the test and see the unhelpful error we get:

```
$ python manage.py test solos.tests.test_views.SoloViewTestCase.test_
basic
Traceback (most recent call last):
...
AttributeError: 'module' object has no attribute 'test_views'
```

Module has no attribute `test_views`?!?!? Yes it does!

This gotcha will turn up if you get used to using dot notation to call single tests. As it turns out, you get this error when you specify down into a module with an `ImportError`. Let's try again, this time running all the tests in the `solos` app:

```
$ python manage.py test solos
Creating test database for alias 'default'...
..E
===================================================================
ERROR: solos.tests.test_views (unittest.loader.ModuleImportFailure)
-------------------------------------------------------------------
Traceback (most recent call last):
...
  File "/Users/kevin/dev/jmad-project/jmad/solos/tests/test_views.py",
line 4, in <module>
    from solos.views import index, SoloDetailView
ImportError: cannot import name 'SoloDetailView'



-------------------------------------------------------------------
Ran 3 tests in 0.002s


FAILED (errors=1)
Destroying test database for alias 'default'...
```

We can work with that. Add `SoloDetailView` to solos/views.py:

```
class SoloDetailView():
    pass
```

Let's try dot notation again:

```
$ python manage.py test solos.tests.test_views.SoloViewTestCase
Creating test database for alias 'default'...
E
======================================================================
ERROR: test_basic (solos.tests.test_views.SoloViewTestCase)
----------------------------------------------------------------------
Traceback (most recent call last):
  File "/Users/kevin/dev/jmad-project/jmad/solos/tests/test_views.py",
line 49, in test_basic
    response = SoloDetailView.as_view()(request, self.drum_solo.pk)
AttributeError: type object 'SoloDetailView' has no attribute 'as_view'


----------------------------------------------------------------------
Ran 1 test in 0.001s

FAILED (errors=1)
Destroying test database for alias 'default'...
```

No attribute `as_view` means I need to subclass my class from Django's `DetailView`:

```
from django.views.generic.detail import DetailView
...
class SoloDetailView(DetailView):
    pass
```

Run the test:

```
$ python manage.py test solos.tests.test_views.SoloViewTestCase
...
AttributeError: 'SoloViewTestCase' object has no attribute
'drum_solo'
```

And we find that we need some test data. I'm going to commit here, as we're about to do some refactoring:

```
$ git commit -am 'Adds test for SoloDetailView and stubs view class'
$ git tag -a ch3-2-stub-solo-view
```

Managing test data

In *Chapter 2, Your First Test-Driven Application*, we added a few objects to our database in a `setUp` method, and we need to do the same here. As a matter of fact, we need to do *exactly* the same thing here.

"Don't Repeat Yourself" (a.k.a. the DRY principle) is a common mantra in the Django community. The idea is that every "thing" (function, value, logic path, etc.) should only exist in one place in the entire system, as we don't want to hunt down every instance of something when we (inevitably) need to change it. It's closely related to the first of the Three Virtues of a GREAT Programmer (`http://threevirtues.com/`): laziness.

In the interest of keeping our test suite as DRY as possible, let's refactor the lines that create test data in such a way that `SoloViewTestCase` can use it as well.

Refactoring

Refactoring is the act of improving the quality of code without changing its functionality. It's an art, and your test suite is the easel on which you'll be working.

Before we touch any existing code, let's run the full test suite so we know exactly where we are:

```
$ python manage.py test

...

Ran 6 tests in 2.474s


FAILED (failures=1, errors=1)
```

I snipped the details, but we got the URL failure in our functional test, and the `AttributeError` in `SoloViewTestCase`. When we have finished refactoring, we should be back in the same spot. Let's start by moving the model creation steps to `setUpClass`.

setUpClass versus setUp

We'd previously used `setUp` to create our models, but let's take this opportunity to optimize a bit. Since `setUp` is called before every single test method, it also gets called in the course of `IndexViewTestCase`. However, `setUpClass` is only called once before the entire test case. And since we're not doing anything with those models besides looking them up, we can leave them in place from test to test.

Edit the top of `IndexViewTestCase` in `solos/tests/test_views.py` like this:

```
class IndexViewTestCase(TestCase):

    def setUp(self):
        self.factory = RequestFactory()

    @classmethod
    def setUpClass(cls):
        super().setUpClass()
        cls.drum_solo = Solo.objects.create(
            instrument='drums',
            artist='Rich',
            track='Bugle Call Rag'
        )
        cls.sax_solo = Solo.objects.create(
            instrument='saxophone',
            artist='Coltrane',
            track='Mr. PC'
        )
```

Two important points on `setUpClass`:

- `setUpClass` is run as a class method, so we have to decorate it with `@classmethod`.

- `django.test.TestCase` (which `IndexViewTestCase` inherits from) uses `setUpClass` for its own purposes, so we have to be sure to call `super().setUpClass()` to pick up that code. Note that this is a significant change from pre-3.0 Python. If you're not on Python 3 yet, replace that line with `super(IndexViewTestCase, cls).setUpClass()`.

Run the tests, and we still get the exact same errors. So far so good.

Speaking of subclassing, since we're working with classes, why don't we subclass the parts of our test cases that are the same? Create a new test case `SolosBaseTestCase` above `IndexViewTestCase` and move the `setUp` and `setUpClass` methods to it. Now we can subclass `IndexViewTestCase` from the new `SolosBaseTestCase`. The new class and the first bit of `IndexViewTestCase` should now look like this:

```
...
class SolosBaseTestCase(TestCase):

    def setUp(self):
```

```
        self.factory = RequestFactory()

    @classmethod
    def setUpClass(cls):
        super().setUpClass()
        cls.drum_solo = Solo.objects
            .create(instrument='drums', artist='Rich',
                    track='Bugle Call Rag')
        cls.sax_solo = Solo.objects
            .create(instrument='saxophone',
                    artist='Coltrane', track='Mr. PC')


class IndexViewTestCase(SolosBaseTestCase):

    def test_index_view_basic(self):
    ...
```

Run the tests again, and we're still the same. No new functionality added, but we've completed the refactor. Let's commit.

```
$ git commit -am 'Refactored test data with setUpClass on
SolosBaseTestCase'
$ git tag -a ch3-3-refactor-test-data
```

DRY testing

Using that test data in `SoloViewTestCase` is now just a matter of subclassing `SolosBaseTestCase`:

```
    class SoloViewTestCase(SolosBaseTestCase):
    ...
```

Run that single test:

```
$ python manage.py test solos.tests.test_views.SoloViewTestCase
Creating test database for alias 'default'...
E
======================================================================
ERROR: test_basic (solos.tests.test_views.SoloViewTestCase)
----------------------------------------------------------------------
Traceback (most recent call last):
```

```
  File "/Users/kevin/dev/jmad-project/jmad/solos/tests/test_views.py",
line 56, in test_basic
    response = SoloDetailView.as_view()(request, self.drum_solo.pk)
...

django.core.exceptions.ImproperlyConfigured: SoloDetailView is missing
a QuerySet. Define SoloDetailView.model, SoloDetailView.queryset, or
override SoloDetailView.get_queryset().


----------------------------------------------------------------------

Ran 1 test in 0.001s


FAILED (errors=1)
Destroying test database for alias 'default'...
```

Now *that* is a helpful error message. It's practically documentation on how to use `DetailView`. The error message offers three options for fixing the error. Let's take its first suggestion and add a `model` attribute to the class.

```
    class SoloDetailView(DetailView):
        model = Solo
```

And now:

```
$ python manage.py test solos.tests.test_views.SoloViewTestCase
Creating test database for alias 'default'...
E
======================================================================
ERROR: test_basic (solos.tests.test_views.SoloViewTestCase)
----------------------------------------------------------------------
Traceback (most recent call last):
  File "/Users/kevin/dev/jmad-project/jmad/solos/tests/test_views.py",
line 56, in test_basic
    response = SoloDetailView.as_view()(request, self.drum_solo.pk)
...

AttributeError: Generic detail view SoloDetailView must be called with
either an object pk or a slug.
```

```
------------------------------------------------------------------
Ran 1 test in 0.001s
```

```
FAILED (errors=1)
```

Here's an implementation oversight on my part—you've got to provide the primary key as a named argument. Wasn't it better to have a test inform us of that, instead an error page? Let's fix it in `solos/tests/test_views.py`:

```
        response = SoloDetailView.as_view()(
            request,
            pk=self.drum_solo.pk
        )
```

Onto the next error:

```
$ python manage.py test solos.tests.test_views.SoloViewTestCase
...
  File "/Users/kevin/.virtualenvs/jmad/lib/python3.4/site-packages/
django/template/loader.py", line 194, in select_template
    raise TemplateDoesNotExist(', '.join(not_found))
django.template.base.TemplateDoesNotExist: solos/solo_detail.html
```

The default template name for a `DetailView` follows the format `<app_name>/<model_name>_detail.html`. It's very easy to change, but we don't have any reason to change it now. Let's add the template so we can move along.

```
$ touch solos/templates/solos/solo_detail.html
$ python manage.py test solos.tests.test_views.SoloViewTestCase
Creating test database for alias 'default'...
.
------------------------------------------------------------------
Ran 1 test in 0.003s
```

```
OK
```

Let's commit that:

```
$ git commit -am 'Adds default functionality for SoloDetailView'
$ git tag -a ch3-4-add-default-solo-view
```

RequestFactory versus TestClient

You may have noticed something funny about the last test: we made a request using the `RequestFactory` instance, passing it a path that does not exist in `urls.py` yet. Why did we have to do that?

Recall that a Django view is simply any function that accepts a request and returns a response. `RequestFactory` creates a bare-bones `WSGIRequest` for the first argument of a view without actually going through the Django framework (URL routing, middleware, and so on). We provide the first argument (path as a keyword) simply because you can't have a `WSGIRequest` without a path. The actual argument is irrelevant, unless you're using it in the course of your view logic (meaning both `/solos/1/` and `/solos/foo/` would have let the test pass).

Using the `WSGIRequest` created by `RequestFactory`, we can call a view like a regular function and test its effects, here setting its returned `HttpResponse` to a variable:

```
response = SoloDetailView.as_view()(request,
    pk=self.drum_solo.pk)
```

To contrast, here's a snippet from a test we wrote in the previous chapter which uses `TestClient` to similar effect. It's in the `test_views.py` file we're currently working in, if you've got your editor open:

```
response = self.client.get('/', {'instrument': 'drums'})
```

This snippet is simulating an HTTP GET request from outside the application. Therefore, if the URL doesn't exist, the response would return a 404 error. It also would have passed through Django's routing, been subjected to any active middleware, and so on.

Which one you decide to use in your tests is up to you. The difference comes down to the amount of isolation you're aiming for in your unit tests. I tend toward `RequestFactory` for this reason. Not only does it ensure that I'm testing exactly what I think I'm testing, but I feel like that isolation makes explicit what the Django framework is actually providing (by virtue of its absence in the tests).

Testing URLs

Let's get our view hooked up to a URL. Add this familiar looking test to `solos/tests/test_urls.py`:

```
def test_solo_details_url(self):
    """
```

```
Test that the URL for SoloDetail resolves to the
correct view function
"""
solo_detail = resolve('/solos/1/')

self.assertEqual(
    solo_detail.func.__name__,
    'SoloDetailView'
)
self.assertEqual(solo_detail.kwargs['pk'], '1')
```

A new wrinkle here: we need to test the `__name__` of the `func` attribute on `solo_detail` to make sure that it's the string version of our CBV's name. `as_view()`, which we use in `urls.py`, returns a function for the URL, hence `solo_detail.func` is a pointer to a function. `solo_detail.func` and `SoloDetailView.as_view()` would not be equal, as they'd be different pointers to the same function.

Does that seem like overkill?

You could argue that testing our implementation of Django's URL routing is unnecessary, and that `test_solo_details_url` is testing configuration, not novel logic. I like to include tests like this for a number reasons:

1. I'm probably the worst regex developer on the planet, and I sleep better knowing mine are tested.

2. If I'm using `RequestFactory` to isolate my view tests, nothing is testing my URL rules if I don't write a specific URL test.

It's up to you to decide if you want the isolation provided by the combination of `RequestFactory` and URL testing, or if the simplicity of using `TestClient` works for you.

Displaying search results

Let's continue by writing the URL for our view and updating the template to use the context from the view. First, run the `solos` tests and we get an error:

```
$ python manage.py test solos
Creating test database for alias 'default'...
..E...
```

```
======================================================================
ERROR: test_solo_details_url (solos.tests.test_urls.SolosURLsTestCase)
----------------------------------------------------------------------

...

django.core.urlresolvers.Resolver404: {'path': 'solo/1/', 'tried':
[[<RegexURLResolver <RegexURLPattern list> (admin:admin) ^admin/>],
[<RegexURLPattern None ^$>]]}
```

Let's add that URL to `jmad/urls.py`:

```
...
from solos.views import SoloDetailView
...

    url(r'^solos/(?P<pk>\d+)/$', SoloDetailView.as_view()),
```

Run the full test suite, and we'll see we're back to all passing except the URL problem in the functional test. Let's save our progress:

```
$ git commit -am 'Adds URL for SoloDetailView'
$ git tag -a ch3-5-add-solo-url
```

Now that we've got a URL to point to, let's link up the search results like we said we would. Update the markup inside the `for` loop in `solos/templates/index.html` like so:

```
<div class="jmad-search-result">
    <a href="/solos/{{ solo.pk }}/">
        {{ solo.track }}: {{ solo.artist }} on
        {{ solo.instrument }}
    </a>
</div>
```

Another test run results in the exact same error we got before. What gives? Turns out, the `<a>` tag is not what we're telling Selenium to click on. Look back at where we were looking for those links in the Selenium tests (line 55 if you're synced up with the repository):

```
second_search_results = self.browser
    .find_elements_by_css_selector('.jmad-search-result')
```

That returns a list of the `div`s of the `jmad-search-result` class. So when we try to do this (on line 59):

```
second_search_results[0].click()
```

we're clicking a `div`, not the `<a>` tag.

Selenium tail-chasing

This is an unfortunately common pattern in Selenium, when you're early on in the project, and your template code is not stable. On the other hand, one might argue that working with Selenium in this way forces you to be judicious about the changes that you make to your templates.

There are ways to mitigate some of this pain. It's often helpful to put repeated element searches into methods on the test case, so that you only have to update them in one place when you update your markup. Let's do that here, since we look up search elements multiple times. Add the following method to `StudentTestCase`:

```
...
def find_search_results(self):
    return self.browser.find_elements_by_css_selector(
        '.jmad-search-result a'
    )
...
```

Then replace the `search_results` and `second_search_results` (lines 47 and now 55) variable definitions with this new method:

```
...
    search_results = self.find_search_results()
...
    second_search_results = self.find_search_results()
...
```

That's another refactor, so let's commit:

```
$ git commit -am 'Adds a tag to search results, small test refactor'
$ git tag -a ch3-6-tag-search-results
```

Building the Solo detail page

When we run the tests again we get another ugly `NoSuchElementException`, which makes sense knowing that we're using a completely blank template. If we take a look at the current state of our model, we can get 'track' and 'artist' on the page. Let's add them in `solos/templates/solo_detail.html`:

```
<p id="jmad-artist">{{ solo.artist }}</p>
<p id="jmad-track">{{ solo.track }}</p>
```

Run the tests again and we get the same error, but at the line where we tell Selenium to look for `#jmad-album`. That's not on the model, and neither are the next two attributes. Let's go back to `solos/tests/test_models.py` and update the test before we add them:

```
class SoloModelTestCase(TestCase):

    def setUp(self):
        self.solo = Solo.objects.create(
            track='Falling in Love with Love',
            artist='Oscar Peterson',
            instrument='piano',
            album='At the Stratford Shakespearean Festival',
            start_time='1:24',
            end_time='4:06'
        )

    def test_solo_basic(self):
        """
        Test the basic functionality of Solo
        """
        self.assertEqual(self.solo.artist, 'Oscar Peterson')
        self.assertEqual(self.solo.end_time, '4:06')
```

Our test fails nicely, as expected:

```
$ python manage.py test solos

=======================================================================
ERROR: test_solo_basic (solos.tests.test_models.SoloModelTestCase)
-----------------------------------------------------------------------
...

TypeError: 'start_time' is an invalid keyword argument for this
function
```

You may get that same type of error but on the `album` or `end_time` field. Regardless, this is an error that's happening in `setUp`. We're trying to give `Solo.objects.create()` a keyword argument that is not a field on the model. Let's update the model in an attempt to get the test to pass:

```
class Solo(models.Model):
    track = models.CharField(max_length=100)
    artist = models.CharField(max_length=100)
```

```
instrument = models.CharField(max_length=50)
album = models.CharField(max_length=200)
start_time = models.CharField(max_length=20, blank=True,
                                            null=True)
end_time = models.CharField(max_length=20, blank=True,
                                          null=True)
```

Now the tests complain about missing columns:

```
$ python manage.py test solos

...

sqlite3.OperationalError: no such column: solos_solo.album


The above exception was the direct cause of the following exception:

...

django.db.utils.OperationalError: no such column: solos_solo.album
```

So let's add the migration, and try again:

```
$ python manage.py makemigrations
```

I'm asked about a default value for `album` as Django makes these migrations. Choose sensible defaults (I picked 'unknown'), but remember that we're probably going to delete and recreate all these migrations before we launch. Now we can run the tests and we'll see that we're all good. Time to commit:

```
$ git commit -am 'Adds album, start_time, end_time fields to Solo'
$ git tag -a ch3-7-add-album-to-solo
```

Is that enough to move us forward on the functional test? Run the whole suite again and you'll see that all the tests pass except the functional test. We first need to update its `setUp` method to use the new fields:

```
def setUp(self):
    self.browser = webdriver.Firefox()
    self.browser.implicitly_wait(2)

    self.solo1 = Solo.objects.create(
        instrument='saxophone',
        artist='John Coltrane',
        track='My Favorite Things',
        album='My Favorite Things'
    )
```

```
        self.solo2 = Solo.objects.create(
            instrument='saxophone',
            artist='Cannonball Adderley',
            track='All Blues',
            album='Kind of Blue',
            start_time='2:06',
            end_time='4:01'
        )
        self.solo3 = Solo.objects.create(
            instrument='saxophone',
            artist='Cannonball Adderley',
            track='Waltz for Debby',
            album='Know What I Mean?'
        )
```

Run the test, and we're in the same spot. Now, try updating `solos/templates/solos/solo_detail.html` with our new fields:

```
<p id="jmad-artist">{{ solo.artist }}</p>
<p id="jmad-track">{{ solo.track }}</p>
<p id="jmad-album">{{ solo.album }}</p>
<p id="jmad-start-time">{{ solo.start_time }}</p>
<p id="jmad-end-time">{{ solo.end_time }}</p>
```

And now the tests:

```
$ python manage.py test
Creating test database for alias 'default'...
.......
----------------------------------------------------------------
Ran 7 tests in 2.750s

OK
Destroying test database for alias 'default'...
```

The functional test passes! Alright! Time for one last victorious commit:

```
$ git commit -am 'Updates solo detail page to use new attributes'
$ git tag -a ch3-8-solo-detail-attrs
```

Summary

In this chapter, we finished our first user story for JMAD, taking the user all the way through the process of searching and visiting a single solo. We learned more about the different tools available in Django's testing toolkit, and when to use them. We also covered a few best practices for keeping your tests maintainable.

In the next chapter we'll add more functionality and do a bit of a refactor.

4

Building Out and Refactoring

In this chapter, we're going to extend our application with new functionality. In the process, we will:

- Refactor many parts of the app and the test suite
- Leverage our test suite to simplify refactoring
- Learn a few more TDD best practices

Improving the application

There are probably a few things about the application that we've built over the last three chapters that you'd like to change. Here are a few improvements I think we should make:

- **Better URLs**: While /solos/1/ is probably easy to remember, it doesn't tell me much about what I might find there. We can do a lot better.

- **Data normalization**: Repeating the album and track on every Solo is hardly DRY. What's more, we'll probably want to show these objects as URLs of their own, as well as list Solos by artist. There are more models that we can add to take advantage of the relational nature of our database backend.

- **More views**: We should give our users the ability to slice and dice the data we're presenting. At a minimum, they should be able to view all the solos on a track, tracks on an album, and solos by a given artist.

A new view

With this in mind, let's take a stab at adding a 'track' view. We can start by updating the functional test with what we expect to see on a Track page. We will totally replace the On the solo page section of the test method. Open jmad/test.py from the repository, and replace from line 67 to the end of the file with the following code:

```
        # On the solo page...
        self.assertEqual(
            self.browser.current_url,
            self.live_server_url +
            '/recordings/kind-of-blue/all-blues/cannonball-
adderley/'
        )

        # he sees the artist...
        self.assertEqual(
            self.browser.find_element_by_css_selector(
                '#jmad-artist').text,
                'Cannonball Adderley'
        )
        # the track title (with a count of solos)...
        self.assertEqual(
            self.browser.find_element_by_css_selector(
                '#jmad-track').text,
                'All Blues [2 solos]'
        )

        # and the album title (with track count) for this solo.
        self.assertEqual(
            self.browser.find_element_by_css_selector(
                '#jmad-album').text,
                'Kind of Blue [3 tracks]'
        )
```

There are a couple of things to notice about these changes:

- We've got a new URL structure to put in place that takes into account the track and album for a given solo, as well as a string representation of the artist's name.

- There are counts of child objects for two parent objects, so we're going to need more models, and more context for our view.

This is enough of change for now; we'll come back to the track and album views in a minute. Let's run the tests:

```
$ python manage.py test
Creating test database for alias 'default'...
......F
======================================================================
FAIL: test_student_find_solos (jmad.tests.StudentTestCase)
----------------------------------------------------------------------
Traceback (most recent call last):
  File "/Users/kevin/dev/jmad-project/jmad/jmad/tests.py", line 69, in
test_student_find_solos
    self.live_server_url + '/recordings/kind-of-blue/all-blues/
cannonball-adderley/')
AssertionError: 'http://localhost:8081/solos/2/' != 'http://
localhost:8081/recordings/kind-of-blue/all-blues/cannonball-adderley/'
- http://localhost:8081/solos/2/
+ http://localhost:8081/recordings/kind-of-blue/all-blues/cannonball-
adderley/


----------------------------------------------------------------------
Ran 7 tests in 2.745s

FAILED (failures=1)
Destroying test database for alias 'default'...
```

As expected, our new URL did not work. Commit the changes we've made so far:

```
$ git commit -am 'Extends functional test for model and URL refactor'
$ git tag -a ch4-1-ext-func-test
```

Pretty URLs

What we're after is a sensible, hierarchical URL structure that gives the user a sense of where they are in the application. We won't implement everything in this chapter, but this is what the user should be able to intuit from the URL in the address bar of the browser:

- `/recordings/`: This is the root list of all recordings available in our application. We'd probably see a paginated list of albums on this page.

- `/recordings/<album-name>/`: This is the root page for a single album. We'll probably have track and musician listings for the album here as well.

- `/recordings/<album-name>/<track-name>/`: This is the root page for a single track. Here, we'd list the solos on the track, perhaps cross-references to other versions of the same song, and more detailed information about the song.

- `/recordings/<album-name>/<track-name>/<artist-name>/`: This is the root page for a solo.

Therefore our test URL (`/recordings/kind-of-blue/all-blues/cannonball-adderley/`) would reference Cannonball Adderley's alto saxophone solo on "All Blues", off of Miles' Davis 1959 record *Kind of Blue*. You could visit `/recordings/kind-of-blue/all-blues/` to see all the solos on that tune, or `/recordings/kind-of-blue/` to get the full track listing.

Back into the TDD cycle

Now that we have an expectedly breaking functional test, let's jump down into our unit tests to get it working. Open `solos/tests/test_urls.py` and update `test_solo_details_url` to be:

```
solo_detail = resolve(
    '/recordings/kind-of-blue/all-blues/cannonball-adderley/'
)

self.assertEqual(solo_detail.func.__name__, 'SoloDetailView')
self.assertEqual(solo_detail.kwargs['album'], 'kind-of-blue')
self.assertEqual(solo_detail.kwargs['track'], 'all-blues')
    self.assertEqual(solo_detail.kwargs['artist'],
                     'cannonball-adderley')
```

Run that test and it fails, as expected:

```
$ python manage.py test solos.tests.test_urls.SolosURLsTestCase.test_solo_details_url

...

==========================================================================
ERROR: test_solo_details_url (solos.tests.test_urls.SolosURLsTestCase)
--------------------------------------------------------------------------

...
```

```
raise Resolver404({'tried': tried, 'path': new_path})
```

```
django.core.urlresolvers.Resolver404: {'tried': [[<RegexURLResolver
<RegexURLPattern list> (admin:admin) ^admin/>], [<RegexURLPattern
None ^solos/(?P<pk>\d+)/$>], [<RegexURLPattern None ^$>]], 'path':
'recordings/kind-of-blue/all-blues/cannonball-adderley/'}
```

To get this test to pass, let's update `jmad/urls.py`. Change the solo URL to this:

```
    ...
        url(r'^solos/(?P<pk>\d+)/$', SoloDetailView.as_view()),
    ...
```

To this:

```
    url(r'^recordings/(?P<album>[\w-]+)/(?P<track>[\w-]+)/(?P<artist>\
    [\w-]+)/$', SoloDetailView.as_view()),
```

There's an unfortunate line break in the preceding snippet. Make sure to not use the \ after `<artist>` in your code. Have a look at the repository for the exact syntax.

We're now capturing three variables in the URL and checking them in the test. We've also switched our pattern matcher from `\d+` (match any number of decimals) to `[\w-]+` (match any number of alphanumeric characters or hyphens). This is necessary since these sections of the URL will now contain the names of tracks and artists, where we formally only had a single primary key.

Run the test, it passes, and we commit:

```
$ git commit -am 'Updates solos URL with album, track info'
$ git tag -a ch4-2-update-solo-url
```

Let's see what that change did to the rest of our test suite:

```
$ python manage.py test
...
AssertionError: 'http://localhost:8081/solos/2/' !=
'http://localhost:8081/recordings/kind-of-blue/all-blues/cannonball-
adderley/'
```

It didn't do much at all really, as we're still in the same spot. Drop `pdb.set_trace()` in `jmad/tests.py` just before the assertion on line 68 and you'll see that the link is still using the old URL. Now would be a great time to add a `get_absolute_url()` method to the `Solo` model. Start by adding it to the template, and our functional test will still fail appropriately:

```
    {% for solo in solos %}
      <div class="jmad-search-result">
        <a href="{{ solo.get_absolute_url }}">
```

```
        {{ solo.track }}: {{ solo.artist }} on {{ solo.instrument }}
      </a>
    </div>
  {% endfor %}
```

Running the tests, we still get the failure at the same spot but now the `current_url` is `http://localhost:8081/?instrument=&artist=Cannonball+Adderley`. Selenium clicked the link, but the `a` tag had no `href` since method calls in Django templates fail silently.

To add the `get_absolute_url()` method, let's start with a new test. Add the following to `solos/tests/test_models.py`:

```
def test_get_absolute_url(self):
    """
    Test that we can build a URL for a solo
    """
      self.assertEqual(
        self.solo.get_absolute_url(),
        '/recordings/at-the-stratford-shakespearean-festival/'
        'falling-in-love-with-love/oscar-peterson/'
      )
```

Note that the URL is one string on two lines, not the second and third argument to `assertEqual`. Running this test we get:

```
$ python manage.py test solos.tests.test_models.SoloModelTestCase.test_
get_absolute_url


AttributeError: 'Solo' object has no attribute 'get_absolute_url'
```

So, add the method to `solos/models.py`:

```
class Solo(models.model):
    ...
    def get_absolute_url(self):
        pass
```

Now, running the test produces `AssertionError: None != '/recordings/at-the-stratford-shakespeare[49 chars]son/'`.

Skipping ahead a bit

I know that I'm eventually going to need to build out more models for the views that I want in the rest of my application, so let's do it now. First we'll finish up `get_absolute_url` with Django's `reverse` function and the values that I know I'm going to need from the solo. Import `reverse`, and add a `return` statement to the method:

```
from django.core.urlresolvers import reverse
...

    def get_absolute_url(self):
        return reverse('solo_detail_view', kwargs={
            'album': self.track.album.slug,
            'track': self.track.slug,
            'artist': self.slug
        })
```

We've jumped ahead a little bit, doing a little bit of *pie in the sky* developing: we're using `reverse` here as if we've got a named URL (we don't… yet), and we're using dot notation to get attributes that we know don't exist yet.

Running the test, we get:

```
$ python manage.py test solos.tests.test_models.SoloModelTestCase.test_
get_absolute_url
...
  File "/Users/kevin/dev/jmad-project/jmad/solos/models.py", line 14,
in get_absolute_url
    'album': self.track.album.slug,
AttributeError: 'str' object has no attribute 'album'
```

Okay, we'll need more models for this. Let's add them to `SoloModelTestCase.setUp`, and update the `Solo` object with what we want the hierarchy to be. Add a couple of imports and the following lines to the `setUp` method in `solos/tests/test_models.py`:

```
from albums.models import Album, Track
...

    def setUp(self):

        self.album = Album.objects.create(
            name='At the Stratford Shakespearean Festival',
            artist='Oscar Peterson Trio',
            slug='at-the-stratford-shakespearean-festival'
```

```
    )

    self.track = Track.objects.create(
        name='Falling in Love with Love',
        album=self.album,
        track_number=1,
        slug='falling-in-love-with-love'
    )

    self.solo = Solo.objects.create(
        track=self.track,
        artist='Oscar Peterson',
        instrument='piano',
        start_time='1:24',
        end_time='4:06',
        slug='oscar-peterson'
    )
```

Trying to run the test at its dotted path will give us `AttributeError` since we've got an unusable import. Let's get that import working.

Starting a new app

This is an important milestone in our TDD journey. We are about to add an entire app to our project, not because we know we need it, but because we are at a point in our user story that demands it. If we'd started this project with what we thought we were going to need, we probably would have created this app and its models right out of the gate. But how would we have known which fields to add? Or what if we had to deal with bugs in the app itself? Or what if we'd added models just to find out later we didn't need them?

Instead, we let our tests drive our code where it needed to go, getting our second app and next models no earlier when we needed them, with tests against regression for the rest of the code. Without further ado, we can now fearlessly add the new app.

```
$ python manage.py startapp albums
```

Then add the following to `albums/models.py`:

```
from django.db import models


class Album(models.Model):
    name = models.CharField(max_length=100)
    artist = models.CharField(max_length=100)
```

```
    slug = models.SlugField()


class Track(models.Model):
    name = models.CharField(max_length=100)
    album = models.ForeignKey(Album)
    track_number = models.PositiveIntegerField(blank=True,
null=True)
    slug = models.SlugField()
```

Run the test again:

```
$ python manage.py test solos.tests.test_models.SoloModelTestCase.test_
get_absolute_url
...
sqlite3.OperationalError: no such table: albums_album


The above exception was the direct cause of the following exception:
...
django.db.utils.OperationalError: no such table: albums_album
```

We need a migration:

```
$ python manage.py makemigrations albums
App 'albums' could not be found. Is it in INSTALLED_APPS?
```

Why, you're right, it's *not* in INSTALLED_APPS. Thanks Django! Fix that in jmad/
settings.py:

```
INSTALLED_APPS = (
    'django.contrib.admin',
    'django.contrib.auth',
    'django.contrib.contenttypes',
    'django.contrib.sessions',
    'django.contrib.messages',
    'django.contrib.staticfiles',
    'solos',
    'albums',
)
```

And try it again:

```
$ python manage.py makemigrations albums
Migrations for 'albums':
  0001_initial.py:
    - Create model Album
```

```
  - Create model Track
```

Test again, and we get a somewhat hard-to-read error:

```
$ python manage.py test solos.tests.test_models.SoloModelTestCase.test_
get_absolute_url

Creating test database for alias 'default'...

E

======================================================================

ERROR: test_get_absolute_url
(solos.tests.test_models.SoloModelTestCase)

----------------------------------------------------------------------

Traceback (most recent call last):
  File "/Users/kevin/dev/jmad-
project/jmad/solos/tests/test_models.py", line 29, in setUp
    slug='oscar-peterson'
  File "/Users/kevin/.virtualenvs/jmad/lib/python3.4/site-
packages/django/db/models/manager.py", line 92, in manager_method
    return getattr(self.get_queryset(), name)(*args, **kwargs)
  File "/Users/kevin/.virtualenvs/jmad/lib/python3.4/site-
packages/django/db/models/query.py", line 370, in create
    obj = self.model(**kwargs)
  File "/Users/kevin/.virtualenvs/jmad/lib/python3.4/site-
packages/django/db/models/base.py", line 454, in __init__
    raise TypeError("'%s' is an invalid keyword argument for this
function" % list(kwargs)[0])
TypeError: 'slug' is an invalid keyword argument for this function
```

The `'slug'` this `TypeError` is referring to is the `slug` field on the `Solo` model, which we forgot to add. Let's fix that now in `solos/models.py`:

```
    class Solo(models.Model):
        ...
        slug = models.SlugField()
```

And run the test:

```
$ python manage.py test solos.tests.test_models.SoloModelTestCase.test_
get_absolute_url

...

django.db.utils.OperationalError: no such column: solos_solo.slug
```

We need another migration. Choose option one and supply a dummy value when the output asks about there being no default for the field:

```
$ python manage.py makemigrations solos
```

Then test:

```
$ python manage.py test solos.tests.test_models.SoloModelTestCase.test_
get_absolute_url
```

```
...

django.core.urlresolvers.NoReverseMatch: Reverse for
'solo_detail_view' with arguments '()' and keyword arguments
'{'track': 'falling-in-love-with-love', 'album': 'at-the-stratford-
shakespearean-festival', 'artist': 'oscar-peterson'}' not found. 0
pattern(s) tried: []
```

We get a `NoReverseMatch` because we're trying to reverse a URL by its name when we haven't given any URLs names yet. Fix this one by naming the URL we're working with in `jmad/urls.py`:

```
...
url(r'^recordings/(?P<album>[\w-]+)/(?P<track>[\w-]+)/
(?P<artist>[\w-]+)/$',
    SoloDetailView.as_view(),
    name='solo_detail_view'),
...
```

Now when we run the test, it passes. Let's check out the full test suite:

```
$ python manage.py test
Creating test database for alias 'default'...
.....E.F
======================================================================
ERROR: test_index_view_returns_solos
(solos.tests.test_views.IndexViewTestCase)
----------------------------------------------------------------------
...

return reverse('solo_detail_view', kwargs={'album':
self.track.album.slug, 'track': self.track.slug,

AttributeError: 'str' object has no attribute 'album'


======================================================================
FAIL: test_student_find_solos (jmad.tests.StudentTestCase)
----------------------------------------------------------------------
```

```
Traceback (most recent call last):
  File "/Users/kevin/dev/jmad-project/jmad/jmad/tests.py", line 54,
in test_student_find_solos
    self.assertGreater(len(search_results), 2)
AssertionError: 0 not greater than 2


----------------------------------------------------------------

Ran 8 tests in 4.858s
```

The functional test is still failing, and we need to update our `index` view test case with new fields for `Solo`. Update the `setUpClass` method in `solos/tests/test_views.py` like so:

```python
@classmethod
def setUpClass(cls):
    super().setUpClass()
    cls.no_funny_hats = Album.objects.create(
        name='No Funny Hats', slug='no-funny-hats')
    cls.bugle_call_rag = Track.objects.create(
        name='Bugle Call Rag', slug='bugle-call-rag',
        album=cls.no_funny_hats)
    cls.drum_solo = Solo.objects.create(
        instrument='drums', artist='Rich',
        track=cls.bugle_call_rag, slug='rich')

    cls.giant_steps = Album.objects.create(
        name='Giant Steps', slug='giant-steps')
    cls.mr_pc = Track.objects.create(
        name='Mr. PC', slug='mr-pc', album=cls.giant_steps)
    cls.sax_solo = Solo.objects.create(
        instrument='saxophone', artist='Coltrane',
        track=cls.mr_pc, slug='coltrane')
```

Run that test now and...

```
$ python manage.py test solos.tests.test_views.IndexViewTestCase.test_
index_view_returns_solos
Creating test database for alias 'default'...
E

...

return reverse('solo_detail_view', kwargs={'album': self.track.album.
slug, 'track': self.track.slug,

AttributeError: 'str' object has no attribute 'album'
```

Wait, what? That's the same error we were getting earlier?

Bonus points for you if you saw this bug coming. We're trying to force a `Track`-shaped peg into a `str`-shaped hole. We forgot to update our `Solo` fields. In `solos/models. py,` update `track` to use a `ForeignKey` relation, and remove the `album` field (which we capture on the related `Track`):

```
from albums.models import Track
...
class Solo(models.Model):
    track = models.ForeignKey(Track)
    artist = models.CharField(max_length=100)
    instrument = models.CharField(max_length=50)
    start_time = models.CharField(max_length=20, blank=True,
                                         null=True)
    end_time = models.CharField(max_length=20, blank=True,
null=True)
    slug = models.SlugField()
```

Our tests tell us we need another migration:

```
$ python manage.py makemigrations solos
Migrations for 'solos':
  0005_auto_20150127_0623.py:
    - Remove field album from solo
    - Alter field track on solo
```

Run the tests now, and we're back to just the functional test failing, but in a new way. Let's take a break and make a commit:

```
$ git add .
$ git commit -m 'Refactors Solo with Album and Track, albums app'
$ git tag -a ch4-3-refactor-solo
```

Much ado about migrations

We sure are building up a lot of migration files. Are these really important, or should we try to consolidate?

At this point you have two options. Since our code hasn't made it anywhere near a production database yet, we can delete all our migrations and let Django rebuild them with `python manage.py makemigrations`. Deleting migrations is a tricky business, and can get you in real trouble if you lose migrations that you might need later. However, at this early stage, I'd feel safe deleting and recreating them.

Updating the functional test

Like the unit tests, we need to add `Albums` and `Tracks` for all the `Solos` in our functional test. Update the `setUp` method in `jmad/test.py`:

```
from albums.models import Album, Track
...
    def setUp(self):
        self.browser = webdriver.Firefox()
        self.browser.implicitly_wait(2)

        self.album1 = Album.objects.create(
            name='My Favorite Things', slug='my-favorite-things')
        self.track1 = Track.objects.create(
            name='My Favorite Things', slug='my-favorite-things',
            album=self.album1)
        self.solo1 = Solo.objects.create(
            instrument='saxophone', artist='John Coltrane',
            track=self.track1, slug='john-coltrane')

        self.album2 = Album.objects.create(
            name='Kind of Blue', slug='kind-of-blue')
        self.track2 = Track.objects.create(
            name='All Blues', slug='all-blues',
            album=self.album2, track_number=4)
        self.solo2 = Solo.objects.create(
            instrument='saxophone', artist='Cannonball Adderley',
            track=self.track2, start_time='4:05', end_time='6:04',
            slug='cannonball-adderley')

        self.album3 = Album.objects.create(
            name='Know What I Mean?', slug='know-what-i-mean')
        self.track3 = Track.objects.create(
            name='Waltz for Debby', slug='waltz-for-debby',
            album=self.album3)
        self.solo3 = Solo.objects.create(
            instrument='saxophone', artist='Cannonball Adderley',
            track=self.track3, slug='cannonball-adderley')
```

After adding these in, we still get an error in the functional test:

```
$ python manage.py test jmad
Creating test database for alias 'default'...
E
```

```
==========================================================================
ERROR: test_student_find_solos (jmad.tests.StudentTestCase)
--------------------------------------------------------------------------
Traceback (most recent call last):
  File "/Users/kevin/dev/jmad-project/jmad/jmad/tests.py", line 79, in
test_student_find_solos
    self.browser.find_element_by_css_selector('#jmad-artist').text,
...
selenium.common.exceptions.NoSuchElementException: Message: Unable to
locate element: {"method":"css selector","selector":"#jmad-artist"}
...
```

Why aren't we getting the `#jmad-artist` element? Let's drop in a `pdb` to see what's up:

```
        ...
        # he sees the artist...
        import pdb;pdb.set_trace()
        self.assertEqual(
            self.browser.find_element_by_css_selector('#jmad-
    artist').text,
            'Cannonball Adderley'
        )
        ...
```

Run the test now and we stop right on top of a big, fat `Internal Server Error` on our solo detail page:

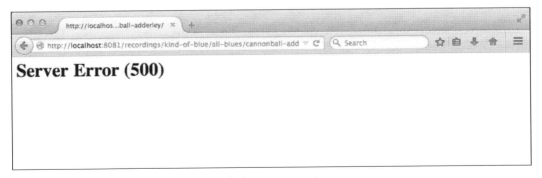

Not the best user experience

Why didn't our unit test catch this?

```
def test_basic(self):
    """
    Test that the solo view returns a 200 response and uses
    the correct template
    """
    request = self.factory.get('/solos/1/')

    response = SoloDetailView.as_view()(request,
        pk=self.drum_solo.pk)
    ...
```

Because it's still doing the look up by primary key, that's why.

Refactoring the index view

Generally speaking, I'm pretty quick to jettison class-based views if the implementation looks like it's going to get weird. Here, we're going to do the lookup with multiple arguments, and getting `DetailView` to do that is just not going to be any fun. Let's go ahead and refactor the test to expect a function-based view. Don't forget to update the import:

```
from solos.views import index, solo_detail

...

    def test_basic(self):
        """

        Test that the solo view returns a 200 response and uses

        The correct template

        """

        request = self.factory.get(
            '/solos/no-funny-hats/bugle-call-rag/buddy-rich/'
        )


        response = solo_detail(
            request,
            album=self.no_funny_hats.slug,
```

```
            track=self.bugle_call_rag.slug,

            artist=self.drum_solo.slug

        )

    . . .
```

Running the tests we see an `ImportError`. Let's refactor in `solos/views.py` now:

```
. . .
# class SoloDetailView(DetailView):
#       model = Solo

def solo_detail():
    pass
```

Try the failing test again:

$ python manage.py test solos.tests.test_views.SoloViewTestCase

. . .

TypeError: solo_detail() got an unexpected keyword argument 'album'

Let's add the arguments, and return a `render_to_response` function (you can get rid of the `DetailView` import too):

```
def solo_detail(request, album, track, artist):
    context = {}
    return render_to_response('solos/solo_detail.html', context)
```

Running the test we get:

AttributeError: 'HttpResponse' object has no attribute 'context_data'

So our test is a little invalidated. Update it with the following:

```
    . . .
        request = self.factory.get(
            '/solos/no-funny-hats/bugle-call-rag/buddy-rich/'
        )

        with self.assertTemplateUsed('solos/solo_detail.html'):
            response = solo_detail(request,
                                   album=self.no_funny_hats.slug,
                                   track=self.bugle_call_rag.slug,
                                   artist=self.drum_solo.slug)

        self.assertEqual(response.status_code, 200)
```

```
        page = response.content.decode()
        self.assertInHTML('<p id="jmad-artist">Buddy Rich</p>', page)
            self.assertInHTML('<p id="jmad-track">Bugle Call Rag</p>',
                                page)
    ...
```

The test now gives us:

**AssertionError: False is not true : Couldn't find '<p id="jmad-artist">
Buddy Rich
</p>' in response**

So let's add some context:

```
    def solo_detail(request, album, track, artist):
        context = {
            'solo': Solo.objects.get(slug=artist, track__slug=track,
                                track__album__slug=album)
        }
        return render_to_response('solos/solo_detail.html', context)
```

And test again:

**AssertionError: False is not true : Couldn't find '<p id="jmad-track">
Bugle Call Rag
</p>' in response**

Now we need to update the template:

```
    <p id="jmad-artist">{{ solo.artist }}</p>
    <p id="jmad-track">{{ solo.track.name }}</p>
    <p id="jmad-album">{{ solo.track.album.name }}</p>
    <p id="jmad-start-time">{{ solo.start_time }}</p>
    <p id="jmad-end-time">{{ solo.end_time }}</p>
```

Finally, the test passes! Let's run the rest of the tests:

$ python manage.py test jmad
Creating test database for alias 'default'...
Traceback (most recent call last):
** File "/Users/kevin/.virtualenvs/jmad/lib/python3.4/site-
packages/django/core/urlresolvers.py", line 364, in urlconf_module**
**   return self._urlconf_module**
**AttributeError: 'RegexURLResolver' object has no attribute
'_urlconf_module'**

```
During handling of the above exception, another exception occurred:
```

```
...
  File "/Users/kevin/dev/jmad-project/jmad/jmad/urls.py", line 4, in
<module>
    from solos.views import SoloDetailView
ImportError: cannot import name 'SoloDetailView'
```

They almost all fail since we now have an `ImportError` in `jmad/urls.py`. Replace the old class-based `SoloDetailView` with `solo_detail` (remove the import):

```
url(r'^recordings/(?P<album>[\w-]+)/(?P<track>[\w-]+)/'
    '(?P<artist>[\w-]+)/$',
    'solos.views.solo_detail',
  name='solo_detail_view'),
```

And try again:

```
$ python manage.py test jmad
```

```
AssertionError: 'All Blues' != 'All Blues [2 solos]'
- All Blues
+ All Blues [2 solos]
```

So close! Let's update the template again:

```
<p id="jmad-track">
  {{ solo.track.name }} [{{solo.track.solo_set.count}} solos]
</p>
```

And add another solo:

```
self.solo4 = Solo.objects.create(instrument='trumpet',
                                 artist='Miles Davis',
                                 track=self.track2,
                                 slug='miles-davis')
```

Running the test shows the same issue for the album track count. Fix it in the template with:

```
<p id="jmad-album">
  {{ solo.track.album.name }}
  [{{solo.track.album.track_set.count}} tracks]
</p>
```

Now in the test:

```
self.track4 = Track.objects.create(name='Freddie Freeloader',
                                   album=self.album2)
self.track5 = Track.objects.create(name='Blue in Green',
                                   album=self.album2)
```

Run the tests:

```
$ python manage.py test
Creating test database for alias 'default'...
...F..F.
=======================================================================
FAIL: test_solo_details_url (solos.tests.test_urls.SolosURLsTestCase)
-----------------------------------------------------------------------
Traceback (most recent call last):
  File "/Users/kevin/dev/jmad-project/jmad/solos/tests/test_urls.py",
line 22, in test_solo_details_url
    self.assertEqual(solo_detail.func.__name__, 'SoloDetailView')
AssertionError: 'solo_detail' != 'SoloDetailView'
- solo_detail
+ SoloDetailView


=======================================================================
FAIL: test_basic (solos.tests.test_views.SoloViewTestCase)
-----------------------------------------------------------------------
Traceback (most recent call last):
  File "/Users/kevin/dev/jmad-
project/jmad/solos/tests/test_views.py", line 72, in test_basic
    self.assertInHTML('<p id="jmad-track">Bugle Call Rag</p>', page)
  File "/Users/kevin/.virtualenvs/jmad/lib/python3.4/site-
packages/django/test/testcases.py", line 671, in assertInHTML
    msg_prefix + "Couldn't find '%s' in response" % needle)
AssertionError: False is not true : Couldn't find '<p id="jmad-
track">
Bugle Call Rag
</p>' in response
```

We broke our URL test, and we're now chasing our tail a bit on the view test. The URL fix is easy. Update `solos/tests/test_urls.py` to:

```
def test_solo_details_url(self):
    ...
    self.assertEqual(solo_detail.func.__name__, 'solo_detail')
```

Then for the view problem, add the count string into the test in `solos/tests/test_urls.py`:

```
    self.assertInHTML('<p id="jmad-track">Bugle Call Rag [1
solo]</p>', page)
```

Now the tests:

```
$ python manage.py test
Creating test database for alias 'default'...
......F.
======================================================================
FAIL: test_basic (solos.tests.test_views.SoloViewTestCase)
----------------------------------------------------------------------
Traceback (most recent call last):
  File "/Users/kevin/dev/jmad-
project/jmad/solos/tests/test_views.py", line 72, in test_basic
    self.assertInHTML('<p id="jmad-track">Bugle Call Rag [1
solo]</p>', page)
  File "/Users/kevin/.virtualenvs/jmad/lib/python3.4/site-
packages/django/test/testcases.py", line 671, in assertInHTML
    msg_prefix + "Couldn't find '%s' in response" % needle)
AssertionError: False is not true : Couldn't find '<p id="jmad-
track">
Bugle Call Rag [1 solo]
</p>' in response
```

But we're still getting the same error... of course, we need to deal with pluralization in the template:

```
<p id="jmad-track">
    {{ solo.track.name }}
    {% with solos=solo.track.solo_set.count %}
        [{{solos}} solo{{ solos|pluralize }}]
    {% endwith %}
</p>
```

```
<p id="jmad-album">
    {{ solo.track.album.name }}
    {% with tracks=solo.track.album.track_set.count %}
        [{{tracks}} track{{ tracks|pluralize }}]
    {% endwith %}
</p>
```

Run the test:

```
$ python manage.py test
Creating test database for alias 'default'...
........
-------------------------------------------------------------------
Ran 8 tests in 2.761s

OK
Destroying test database for alias 'default'...
```

And done. Let's commit:

```
$ git commit -am 'Refactors solo detail view to use new models'
$ git tag -a ch4-4-refactor-solo-view
```

Summary

In this chapter we changed the application with TDD, refactoring both our test suite and application code for maintainability. We also covered options for dealing with migrations.

In the next chapter we'll explore further the controls available in the Selenium web driver by building out the Django admin site.

5

User Stories As Code

We've made a lot of progress over the last three chapters: we've added views, models, templates, and URLs for a pretty solid minimally viable product. In this chapter, we're going to learn more about Selenium and `LiveServerTestCase` by writing a new functional test for a second user story. We'll learn about:

- More of the browser actions available in the Python bindings for Selenium
- Why it's crucial for your functional tests to track user experience
- Using the Django admin site to fulfill staff user stories

A second user story

This chapter will focus on the art of enshrining a user story in an executable functional test. Nothing will give you more confidence as a developer than checking every single known user interaction in your project after any change you make. Time invested in having an accurate, comprehensive, and narrative version of your user story that you can run as a functional test will pay big dividends as your project grows.

After the last three chapters, we've got a pretty solid foundation in place for the end user's experience. But what about the folks that are going to be populating our website? The user stories for staff users (those with access to add, edit, and delete content) are at least as important if we plan on getting much data added to this site. Here's a user story for a "Staff User":

 As a Staff User, I want to add Albums, Tracks, and Solos to the database so that they can be presented as content.

As you probably know, Django comes with a great admin site that takes very little code to get up running. We'll use that to provide an interface to add Albums, Tracks, and Solos to our application. To get started, let's add a narrative version of the new user story as comments in jmad/test.py:

```
. . .
        def test_staff_can_add_content(self):
            """
            Tests that a 'staff' user can access the admin and
            add Albums, Tracks, and Solos
            """
            # Bill would like to add a record and a number of
            # solos to JMAD. He visits the admin site

            # He can tell he's in the right place because of the
            # title of the page

            # He enters his username and password and submits the
            # form to log in

            # He sees links to Albums, Tracks, and Solos

            # He clicks on Albums and sees all of the Albums that
            # have been added so far

            # Going back to the home page, he clicks the Tracks
            # link and sees the Tracks that have been added.
            # They're ordered first by Album, then by track
            # number.

            # He adds a track to an album that already exists

            # He adds another track, this time on an album that
            # is not in JMAD yet

            # After adding the basic Track info, he clicks on the
            # plus sign to add a new album.

            # The focus shifts to the newly opened window, where
            # he sees an Album form

            # After creating the Album, he goes back to finish
            # the Track
```

```
    # He goes back to the root of the admin site and
    # clicks on 'Solos'

    # He sees Solos listed by Album, then Track, then
    # start time

    # He adds a Solo to a Track that already exists

    # He then adds a Solo for which the Track and Album
    # do not yet exist

    # He adds a Track from the Solo page

    # He adds an Album from the Track popup

    # He finishes up both parent objects, and saves the
    # Solo
```

Activating the Django admin site

Just as we did in *Chapter 2, Your First Test-Driven Application*, we'll start with just a couple of actions and a placeholder. Let's have our functional test look for the Django admin at the /admin/ URL, confirm that we can see the title of the page, and move our placeholder to fail afterward:

```
    # Bill would like to add a record and a number of solos to
    # JMAD. He visits the admin site
    admin_root = self.browser.get(
        self.live_server_url + '/admin/')

    # He can tell he's in the right place because of the title
    self.assertEqual(self.browser.title,
                    'Log in | Django site admin')
    self.fail('Incomplete Test')
```

We don't have to do any work since the admin site is already set up (check out jmad/urls.py):

```
$ python manage.py test
jmad.tests.StudentTestCase.test_staff_can_add_content

...

AssertionError: Incomplete Test
```

This test will make it to the placeholder, but we'll get a really ugly error message ending in `TypeError: unsupported operand type(s) for +=: 'NoneType' and 'str'`. Since our tests are not running in `DEBUG` mode, the static files aren't being served by the Django development server. You may have noticed an unstyled admin page as Firefox whizzed by. Drop in a debugger (`import pdb;pdb.set_trace()`)to take a closer look if you like.

The unstyled admin login screen

Let's do as little configuration as possible to clean up this test. First, we add a `STATIC_ROOT` setting to `jmad/settings.py`:

```
STATIC_ROOT = os.path.join(BASE_DIR, 'static')
```

`BASE_DIR` is defined higher up as the directory of the settings file (generated when we originally created our Django project). Now, we can run `collectstatic`:

```
$ python manage.py collectstatic

You have requested to collect static files at the destination
location as specified in your settings:

    /Users/kevin/dev/jmad-project/jmad/static

This will overwrite existing files!
Are you sure you want to do this?

Type 'yes' to continue, or 'no' to cancel: yes
Copying '/Users/kevin/.virtualenvs/jmad/lib/python3.4/site-packages/
django/contrib/admin/static/admin/css/base.css'
...
62 static files copied to '/Users/kevin/dev/jmad-project/jmad/static'.
```

Run the tests again and you'll see a flash of the familiar Django admin and no error in the terminal output:

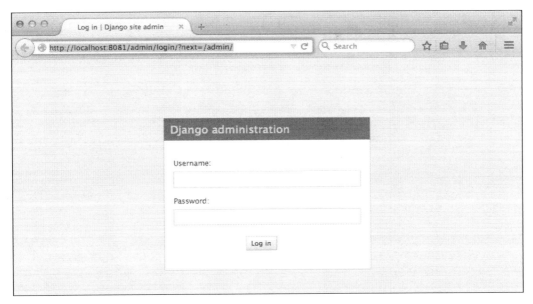

That's more like it.

Let's commit our clean, stubbed test:

```
$ git commit -am 'Initial staff functional test, static settings'
$ git tag -a ch5-1-init-staff-func-test
```

Signing in with Selenium

Next we need to log in to the admin site: to do that, we'll need an admin user. Let's add one in `setUp` and log him in (don't forget to move the placeholder):

```
from django.contrib.auth import get_user_model
...
    def setUp(self):
        ...
        self.admin_user = \
            get_user_model().objects.create_superuser(
                username='bill',
                email='bill@example.com',
                password='password'
            )
    ...
```

```
def test_staff_can_add_content(self):
    ...
    # He enters his username and password and submits the
    # form to log in
    login_form = self.browser.find_element_by_id(
        'login-form')
    login_form.find_element_by_name('username').\
        send_keys('bill')

    login_form.find_element_by_name('password').\
        send_keys('password')
    login_form.find_element_by_css_selector(
        '.submit-row input').click()
    self.fail('Incomplete Test')
```

We use `find_element_by_id` to find the form on the page, and then `find_element_by_name` to interact with the individual pieces. Even though we're testing generated code (the Django admin interface), this pattern ensures a couple of important things for us:

- We guarantee that we have unique name attributes for each form element. This way we know we'll be perfectly clear when we POST our forms back to the server.

- When we find the form by `id` first but look up the form elements by `name`, we're allowing ourselves to standardize form field `name` in our UI. This is in case if we ever need more than one form with the same elements in the DOM (for example, a login form in a header that's hidden via JavaScript, but still present on our `/login/` page)

Run the test and you will see that we make it back to the placeholder. Now we can look for some links:

```
# He sees links to Albums, Tracks, and Solos
albums_links = self.browser.\
    find_elements_by_link_text('Albums')

self.assertEqual(
    albums_links[0].get_attribute('href'),
    self.live_server_url + '/admin/albums/'
)

self.assertEqual(
    albums_links[1].get_attribute('href'),
    self.live_server_url + '/admin/albums/album/'
)
```

```
self.assertEqual(
    self.browser.\
        find_element_by_link_text('Tracks').\
            get_attribute('href'),
    self.live_server_url + '/admin/albums/track/'
)

solos_links = self.browser.\
    find_elements_by_link_text('Solos')
self.assertEqual(
    solos_links[0].get_attribute('href'),
    self.live_server_url + '/admin/solos/'
)
self.assertEqual(
    solos_links[1].get_attribute('href'),
    self.live_server_url + '/admin/solos/solo/'
)
self.fail('Incomplete Test')
```

We're using `find_elements_by_link_text` and `find_element_by_link_text` to access links by their visible text. The plural form of the locator gets both 'Albums' links on the page. Since the list honors the order the elements appear on the page, we're also testing for that order. We're following the Django best practice of naming our apps based on the plural form of the major model they contain, which is why we'll wind up with two 'Albums' links and two 'Solos' links.

 Whenever possible, try to make Selenium act as much like a human as you can. That means finding links by their text, using `click()` to click on submit buttons instead of `submit()` forms, and using the browser's navigation. You're trying to empathize with the user, so don't cut corners. If Selenium is having trouble finding a link by its text, there's probably a good chance your users will have that same problem.

All of the `find_elements_by_*` selectors return lists of elements in the same order they appear on the page. Therefore we look for the link to `http://localhost:8081/admin/albums/` (the admin root of the albums app) to be the first, and `http://localhost:8081/admin/albums/album/` (the actual `Album` model admin) to be the second.

Run the tests:

```
$ python manage.py test jmad.tests.StudentTestCase.test_staff_can_add_
content

...

Traceback (most recent call last):
  File "/Users/kevin/dev/jmad-project/jmad/jmad/tests.py", line 137,
in test_staff_can_add_content
    albums_links[0].get_attribute('href'),
IndexError: list index out of range
```

`find_elements_by_*` selectors always return lists; empty ones if no elements match the search. Let's get that working by first editing `albums/admin.py`:

```
from django.contrib import admin

from .models import Album, Track


admin.site.register(Album)
admin.site.register(Track)
```

Now the test gives us another `IndexError`, this time for the `solo_links` list. Edit `solos/admin.py` to get this test to pass:

```
from django.contrib import admin

from .models import Solo


admin.site.register(Solo)
```

That's enough to get back to the placeholder. We haven't done a commit since we've added this and the login action, so now's a good time.

```
$ git commit -am 'Staff login, initial model admin registration'
$ git tag -a ch5-2-staff-login
```

Let's go to the next action:

```
    # He clicks on Albums and sees all of the Albums that
    # have been added so far
    albums_links[1].click()

    self.assertEqual(
        self.browser.find_element_by_link_text(
```

```
                'Know What I Mean?').get_attribute('href'),
        self.live_server_url + '/admin/albums/album/3/'
    )

    self.assertEqual(
        self.browser.find_element_by_link_text(
            'Kind of Blue').get_attribute('href'),
        self.live_server_url + '/admin/albums/album/2/'
    )

    self.assertEqual(
        self.browser.find_element_by_link_text(
            'My Favorite Things').get_attribute('href'),
        self.live_server_url + '/admin/albums/album/1/'
    )
    self.fail('Incomplete Test')
```

None of this passes (we get our old friend `Unable to locate element`). Halt the test with the debugger and we'll see that each album is represented by 'Album object'. The Django admin uses the `__str__` method on our models. If we don't define our own, this is the default we get. Let's fix our `Album` model in `albums/models.py`:

```
class Album(models.Model):
    ...
    def __str__(self):
        return self.name
```

We're simply returning the value of the `Album` object's `name` field. Run the tests, and we're back to the placeholder. Let's commit:

```
$ git commit -am 'Adds string representation for Track'
$ git tag -a ch5-3-track-str-rep
```

Configuring the Django admin model list display

The next comment in our functional test hints at a more advanced configuration. Here are the assertions that we need:

```
# Going back to the home page, he clicks the Tracks link and
# sees the Tracks that have been added. They're ordered first
# by Album, then by track number.
self.browser.find_element_by_css_selector(
    '#site-name a').click()
self.browser.find_element_by_link_text('Tracks').click()
```

```
track_rows = self.browser.find_elements_by_css_selector(
                '#result_list tr')

self.assertEqual(track_rows [1].text,
                'Kind of Blue Freddie Freeloader 2')
self.assertEqual(track_rows [2].text,
                'Kind of Blue Blue in Green 3')
self.assertEqual(track_rows [3].text,
                'Kind of Blue All Blues 4')
self.assertEqual(track_rows [4].text,
                'Know What I Mean? Waltz for Debby (None)')
self.assertEqual(track_rows [5].text,
                'My Favorite Things My Favorite Things \ (None)')
self.fail('Incomplete Test')
```

This block of assertions is implying a lot of configuration. First, we're going to show the Track's `album` attribute, then its `name`, and then its `track_number` if it has one. We check for the whole row as one string with spaces, because that's what Selenium will give us when we ask for the `.text` of a multi-cell `<tr>` tag.

We list the track objects in order of their `album` attribute (instead of `id`, which is the default). Note that we start checking at index `one`, because the first `<tr>` will be the heading row.

When we run our test, we get:

```
AssertionError: 'Track' != 'Kind of Blue Freddie Freeloader 2'
- Track object
+ Kind of Blue Freddie Freeloader 2
```

As expected, each track is represented by the default __str__. What if we add a __str__ method to `Track` as we did to `Album`?

```
class Track(models.Model):
...
    def __str__(self):
        return self.name
```

The test now throws a different error:

```
AssertionError: 'Blue in Green' != 'Kind of Blue Freddie Freeloader
2'
- Blue in Green
+ Kind of Blue Freddie Freeloader 2
```

We do get a track name, but not the right one. Let's set some ordering on the model:

```
class Track(models.Model):
    ...
    class Meta:
        ordering = ['album', 'track_number']
```

Now when we run the tests we get:

AssertionError: 'My Favorite Things' != 'Kind of Blue Freddie Freeloader 2'

- My Favorite Things

+ Kind of Blue Freddie Freeloader 2

Since `album` is a `ForeignKey` to Album, we're picking up its ordering, which we never changed from the default. Let's alphabetize it now:

```
class Album(models.Model):
    ...
    class Meta:
        ordering = ['name']
```

Run our test:

AssertionError: 'Blue in Green' != 'Kind of Blue Freddie Freeloader 2'

- Blue in Green

+ Kind of Blue Freddie Freeloader 2

`Blue in Green` is on the right first album, but we need to add track numbers to our fixtures. They're in the `setUp` method:

```
self.track4 = Track.objects.create(
            name='Freddie Freeloader',
            album=self.album2,
            track_number=2
        )
self.track5 = Track.objects.create(
            name='Blue in Green',
            album=self.album2,
            track_number=3
        )
```

Run the test one more time:

```
AssertionError: 'Freddie Freeloader' != 'Kind of Blue Freddie
Freeloader 2'
- Freddie Freeloader
+ Kind of Blue Freddie Freeloader 2
```

We've now gone as far as the model's `Meta` options can take us. To get the rest of the Track's data in that `<tr>` tag, we need a customized `ModelAdmin`. Update `albums/admin.py` with this:

```
class TrackAdmin(admin.ModelAdmin):
    model = Track
    list_display = ('album', 'name', 'track_number')
...
    admin.site.register(Track, TrackAdmin).
```

Don't forget to add `TrackAdmin` to the register line at the bottom. Try the test now and we make it back to the placeholder.

```
$ git commit -am 'Adds str, ordering, and columns for Track admin'
$ git tag -a ch5-4-add-track-columns
```

Adding content via the Django admin

Our next task is our first chance to add data to the admin site:

```
# He adds a track to an album that already exists
self.browser.find_element_by_link_text('Add track').click()
track_form = self.browser.find_element_by_id('track_form')
track_form.find_element_by_name('name').send_keys('So What')
track_form.find_element_by_name('album').\
    find_elements_by_tag_name('option')[1].click()
track_form.find_element_by_name('track_number').\
    send_keys('1')
track_form.find_element_by_name('slug').send_keys('so-what')
track_form.find_element_by_css_selector(
    '.submit-row input').click()

self.assertEqual(
    self.browser.find_elements_by_css_selector(
        '#result_list tr')[1].text,
    'Kind of Blue So What 1'
)
self.fail('Incomplete Test')
```

We're working with a form again, but this one has a dropdown `<select>`, which requires some special care in Selenium. There are a number of ways to get to the `<option>` elements, but I prefer two chained `find_` calls. It may be more verbose, but it's a little easier to understand, and is more similar to what a real user does (clicking the `<select>` first, then clicking the desired `<option>`).

This bit of the functional test was exercising functionality that was already activated, so we're back to the placeholder.

Why are we writing tests for the stuff that already works?

It may seem like overkill, or at the very least not "test-driven" to write tests for something as basic as adding data to the Django admin. One might argue that we're testing the inner workings of Django's admin, not our own code. In this case, however, I'm taking the extra step for two reasons. One, this functionality is absolutely crucial to the success of this application. Two, the backend is just as likely to be updated as the frontend, and I want to guard against regressions as we continue to build new features.

Building further on the last block, let's try to add a `Track` with an `Album` (even though it's not in the database yet):

```
# He adds another track, this time on an album that is not in
# JMAD yet
self.browser.find_element_by_link_text('Add track').click()
track_form = self.browser.find_element_by_id('track_form')
track_form.find_element_by_name('name').\
    send_keys('My Funny Valentine')


# After adding the basic Track info, he clicks on the plus
# sign to add a new album.
track_form.find_element_by_id('add_id_album').click()


# The focus shifts to the newly opened window, where he sees
# an Album form
self.browser.switch_to.window(self.browser.window_handles[1])
album_form = self.browser.find_element_by_id('album_form')
album_form.find_element_by_name('name').send_keys('Cookin\'')
album_form.find_element_by_name('artist').\
    send_keys('Miles Davis Quintet')
album_form.find_element_by_name('slug').send_keys('cookin')
album_form.find_element_by_css_selector(
    '.submit-row input').click()
```

```
# After creating the Album, he goes back to finish the Track
self.browser.switch_to.window(self.browser.window_handles[0])
track_form = self.browser.find_element_by_id('track_form')
track_form.find_element_by_name('track_number').\
    send_keys('1')
track_form.find_element_by_name('slug').\
    send_keys('my-funny-valentine')
track_form.find_element_by_css_selector(
    '.submit-row input').click()

self.assertEqual(
    self.browser.find_elements_by_css_selector(
        '#result_list tr'
    )[1].text,
    'Cookin\' My Funny Valentine 1'
)
self.fail('Incomplete Test')
```

Notice `switch_to.window`, which takes as its first argument a handle ID to a window that Selenium can access. We use `window_handles` to get a list of these IDs. `window_handles` will maintain the order in which the windows were opened, so we can use the index of the window to move back and forth.

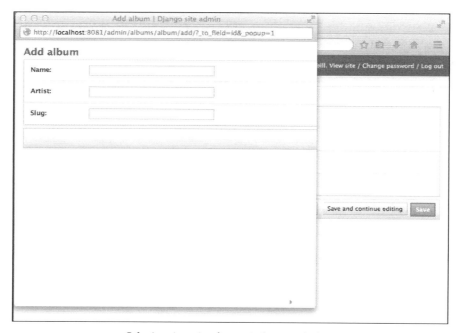

Selenium jumping from window to window

We now run our tests and they should pass, switching between open windows to add the records. Moving on, let's add a `Solo`, `Track`, and `Album` all in one shot:

```
# He goes back to the root of the admin site and clicks on
# 'Solos'
self.browser.find_element_by_css_selector(
    '#site-name a').click()
self.browser.find_elements_by_link_text('Solos')[1].click()

# He's sees Solos listed by Album, then Track, then start
# time
solo_rows = self.browser.find_elements_by_css_selector(
                '#result_list tr')

self.assertEqual(solo_rows[1].text,
                'All Blues Miles Davis 1:46-4:04')
self.assertEqual(solo_rows[2].text,
                'All Blues Cannonball Adderley 4:05-6:04')
self.assertEqual(solo_rows[3].text.strip(),
                'Waltz for Debby Cannonball Adderley')
self.assertEqual(solo_rows[4].text.strip(),
                'My Favorite Things John Coltrane')
self.fail('Incomplete Test')
```

Since we haven't done anything more than set up the default implementation, the test fails.

```
python manage.py test jmad.tests.StudentTestCase.test_staff_can_add_content
...
AssertionError: 'Solo object' != 'All Blues Miles Davis 1:46-4:04'
- Solo object
+ All Blues Miles Davis 1:46-4:04
```

It looks like our `list_display` for `Solos` is a bit lacking. Let's update it. In `solos/admin.py`:

```
class SoloAdmin(admin.ModelAdmin):
    model = Solo
    list_display = ['track', 'artist', 'get_duration']
...
admin.site.register(Solo, SoloAdmin)
```

We haven't defined `get_duration`, so when we run the tests we get an `IndexError` in the terminal and a `Server Error (500)` in the browser when it tries to serve the Solos index. Add a quick test to `SoloModelTestCase` in `solos/tests/test_models.py` to define what we want the function to do:

```
...

    def test_get_duration(self):
        """
        Test that we can print the duration of a Solo
        """
        self.assertEqual(self.solo.get_duration(),
                         '1:24-4:06')
```

This test raises an `AttributeError`, since we haven't added it to the model yet. Let's do that now in `solos/models.py`:

```
class Solo(models.Model):
...

    def get_duration(self):
        duration_string = ''
        if self.start_time and self.end_time:
            duration_string = '{}-{}'.format(self.start_time,
                                             self.end_time)
        return duration_string
```

That gets the model test to pass. Back in the functional test, an assertion fails since our fixtures aren't up to date:

```
AssertionError: 'All Blues Miles Davis ' != 'All Blues Miles Davis 1:46-
4:04'
```

Fix that in `setUp`:

```
    ...

    self.solo4 = Solo.objects.create(
        instrument='trumpet', artist='Miles Davis',
        track=self.track2, slug='miles-davis',
        start_time='1:46', end_time='4:04')
```

At this point, the test gives us similar ordering errors just as in our earlier `Track` section:

```
AssertionError: 'Waltz for Debby Cannonball Adderley ' != 'All Blues
Cannonball Adderley 4:05-6:04'

- Waltz for Debby Cannonball Adderley

+ All Blues Cannonball Adderley 4:05-6:04
```

Again update `solos/models.py`:

```
class Solo(models.Model):
...
    class Meta:
        ordering = ['track', 'start_time']
```

Now that we've got our `list_display` and ordering set, our test will make it back to the placeholder. Let's commit that:

```
$ git commit -am 'Improves track listing, further tests content mgmt'
$ git tag -a ch5-5-improve-track-listing
```

Finishing up

Let's add a `Solo`:

```
# He adds a Solo to a Track that already exists
self.browser.find_element_by_link_text('Add solo').click()
solo_form = self.browser.find_element_by_id('solo_form')
solo_form.find_element_by_name('track').\
        find_elements_by_tag_name('option')[6].click()
solo_form.find_element_by_name('artist').\
        send_keys('McCoy Tyner')
solo_form.find_element_by_name('instrument').\
        send_keys('Piano')
solo_form.find_element_by_name('start_time').\
        send_keys('2:19')
solo_form.find_element_by_name('end_time').\
        send_keys('7:01')
solo_form.find_element_by_name('slug').\
        send_keys('mcoy-tyner')
solo_form.find_element_by_css_selector(
            '.submit-row input').click()

self.assertEqual(
    self.browser.find_elements_by_css_selector(
        '#result_list tr')[5].text,
    'My Favorite Things McCoy Tyner 2:19-7:01')
self.fail('Incomplete Test')
```

This makes it back to the placeholder without issue. Now on to the grand finale—adding a `Solo` for which the `Track` and `Album` do not yet exist. This will essentially take us through the entire admin process:

```python
# He then adds a Solo for which the Track and Album do not
# yet exist
self.browser.find_element_by_link_text('Add solo').click()
solo_form = self.browser.find_element_by_id('solo_form')

# He adds a Track from the Solo page
solo_form.find_element_by_id('add_id_track').click()
self.browser.switch_to.window(self.browser.window_handles[1])
track_form = self.browser.find_element_by_id('track_form')
track_form.find_element_by_name('name').\
    send_keys('In Walked Bud')

# He adds an Album from the Track popup
track_form.find_element_by_id('add_id_album').click()
self.browser.switch_to.window(self.browser.window_handles[2])
album_form = self.browser.find_element_by_id('album_form')
album_form.find_element_by_name('name').\
    send_keys('Misterioso')
album_form.find_element_by_name('artist').\
    send_keys('Thelonious Monk Quartet')
album_form.find_element_by_name('slug').\
    send_keys('misterioso')
album_form.find_element_by_css_selector(
    '.submit-row input').click()

# He finishes up both parent objects, and saves the Solo
self.browser.switch_to.window(self.browser.window_handles[1])
track_form = self.browser.find_element_by_id('track_form')
track_form.find_element_by_name('track_number').\
    send_keys('4')
track_form.find_element_by_name('slug').\
    send_keys('in-walked-bud')
track_form.find_element_by_css_selector(
    '.submit-row input').click()

self.browser.switch_to.window(self.browser.window_handles[0])
solo_form = self.browser.find_element_by_id('solo_form')
solo_form.find_element_by_name('artist').\
    send_keys('Johnny Griffin')
solo_form.find_element_by_name('instrument').\
```

```
        send_keys('Tenor Saxophone')
    solo_form.find_element_by_name('start_time').\
        send_keys('0:59')
    solo_form.find_element_by_name('end_time').\
        send_keys('6:21')
    solo_form.find_element_by_name('slug').\
        send_keys('johnny-griffin')
    solo_form.find_element_by_css_selector(
        '.submit-row input').click()

    self.assertEqual(
        self.browser.find_elements_by_css_selector(
            '#result_list tr')[4].text,
        'In Walked Bud Johnny Griffin 0:59-6:21'
    )
```

Run the full test suite and behold the majesty of two entirely automated user stories!

```
$ python manage.py test
Creating test database for alias 'default'...
.........
---------------------------------------------------------------
Ran 10 tests in 10.272s


OK
Destroying test database for alias 'default'...
```

Commit our newly completed feature.

```
$ git commit -am 'Completes functional test for staff user story'
$ git tag -a ch5-6-complete-staff-func-test
```

Summary

In this chapter, we covered the importance of automated testing of the user's experience in the browser. We learned a few more of the controls available in the Python Selenium bindings, and used Test-Driven Development to build out the Django admin. In the next chapter, we'll use TDD to build an integration with an external API.

6
No App Is an Island

In this chapter, we'll learn how to mock responses for external APIs as we write functions that integrate with other systems over the Internet. We'll talk about:

- Why we'd need to mock an external system
- `unittest.mock` and its associated utilities
- Patterns for TDD with external API dependencies

What is a mock?

Permit me an American sports metaphor: imagine you're a baseball player who wants to learn to hit curveballs. To do so, you'd need to practice. In the normal course of a game, a pitcher would throw curveballs (as well as other pitches) to you, so you could ask a pitcher to practice with you.

This may work in the short term, but what if the pitcher isn't always available when you want to practice? What if she's only able to throw you a certain number of pitches before she tires out? What if you need to practice hitting curveballs from a left-handed pitcher and she's a righty? Or maybe you want to practice curveballs thrown to a very specific part of the strike zone, but she isn't accurate enough to throw a strike every time?

You might represent the main parts of this system in Python like this:

```
class Pitch:

    def __init__(self, velocity, accuracy, trajectory):
        self.velocity = velocity
        self.accuracy = accuracy
        self.trajectory = trajectory # 'fastball' or 'curve'
```

```
class Pitcher:

    handedness = 'left'

    def throw_curveball(self):
        import random
        return Pitch(velocity=random.randint(0, 100),
                     accuracy=random.randint(0, 100),
                     trajectory='curve')


class Batter:

    def swing(self, pitch):
        # TODO: hit a curveball
        return
```

You are a `Batter` object, and the pitcher would be a `Pitcher`. A `Pitcher` can `throw_curveball`, which returns a `Pitch` of variable velocity and accuracy. The `swing` method of `Batter` will accept a `Pitch` (as returned by `throw_curveball`), but we need to develop the method to hit it.

In order to overcome the problems practicing with a human pitcher (inaccuracy, stamina, handedness), you could replace her with a pitching machine, configured to throw curveballs in the same part of the strike zone with no stamina limit, toggling for handedness if you needed.

A **mock** can mimic an object for the duration of a single test, allowing you to define how methods on that object react. In the previous example, we might mock out the `Pitcher` object in tests for `Batter.swing`. We'd set the exact velocity and accuracy of the `Pitch` returned by `throw_curveball`, and write one test for each `handedness` configuration, thereby accounting for the inaccuracy and fixed configuration of the real `Pitch` object.

Mocks are handy for testing around the parts of your project that are hard or impossible to control, like an external API. Let's integrate such an API into JMAD, writing mocked tests first along the way.

MusicBrainz

You've undoubtedly realized at this stage in the game that very little of what we're building is novel. In just a couple of decades, the Internet has done a pretty solid job of collecting most of humanity's written information. Jazz artists, albums, and tracks are represented in several systems, some of which are already integrated. In the interest of not reinventing the wheel (and avoiding a lot of data entry), we should find a preexisting database that can get us this baseline data. That way we can focus our efforts on adding the solo details to Earth's hive mind. Enter MusicBrainz.

MusicBrainz (`https://musicbrainz.org/`) (hereafter MB) is an open database of music and recording information. The data is added and edited by volunteers, and is freely available for any type of use. The database is most commonly used to identify digital recordings (think Spotify), but they also expose the core data via a RESTful API, including search and standard lookup endpoints.

If that wasn't great enough, there's already a Python library we can use to access the API. `musicbrainzngs` (`https://github.com/alastair/python-musicbrainzngs`) is a pip-installable package that abstracts the MB API into Python functions that return dictionaries.

Digging around in the MusicBrainz sandbox

Before we dive back into our test suite, let's have a peek around the MB API to get a feel for how it works. Start by installing `musicbrainzngs`:

```
$ pip install musicbrainzngs
```

Now open up `http://python-musicbrainzngs.readthedocs.org/` in your browser, start up your interpreter, and try out some of the methods:

```
$ python
>>> import musicbrainzngs as mb
>>> mb.set_useragent('Kevin Test App - kevin@kevinharvey.net',
>>>                   version='0.0.1')
```

The `set_useragent()` bit sets a header for each subsequent API call. MB requires this so it can keep track of who or what is communicating with it. Most external APIs require some sort of identification like this, either for authorization or in the event they need to throttle the number of calls made. This is often accomplished by a header on each request, as is the case here.

Let's try a search: \

```
>>> mb.search_artists('Oscar Peterson')
{'artist-count': 577, 'artist-list': [{'sort-name': 'Peterson,
Oscar', 'tag-list': [{'count': '1', 'name': 'piano jazz'}, {'count':
'1', 'name': 'death by kidney failure'}, {'count': '2', 'name':
'jazz'}, {'count': '1', 'name': 'canadian'}], 'life-span': {'ended':
'true',

...
```

I've snipped quite a lot of output here. The big blob of text you see in your terminal is the first 25 of 577 artists that match the search phrase `Oscar Peterson`, ordered by relevance. Let's clean up the first result so we can read it:

```
>>> mb.search_artists('Oscar Peterson')
{
    'artist-count': 577,
    'artist-list': [
    {
        'sort-name': 'Peterson, Oscar',
        'tag-list': [
            {
                'count': '1',
                'name': 'piano jazz'
            }, {
                'count': '1',
                'name': 'death by kidney failure'
            }, {
                'count': '2',
                'name': 'jazz'
            }, {
                'count': '1',
                'name': 'canadian'
            }
        ],
        'life-span': {
            'ended': 'true',
            'end': '2007-12-23',
            'begin': '1925-08-15'
```

```
    },
    'end-area': {
      'sort-name': 'Ontario',
      'id': '2747553f-b44d-44c4-a7c3-b67412b6f10b',
      'name': 'Ontario'
    },
    'ext:score': '100',
    'id': 'ed801bdd-f057-41c0-94fb-76cb5676cd59',
    'begin-area': {
      'sort-name': 'Montreal',
      'id': 'c3cc624e-b963-49cf-ad0b-e318cb341963',
      'name': 'Montreal'
    },
    'gender': 'male',
    'country': 'CA',
    'alias-list': [
      {
        'sort-name': 'Oscar Petersen',
        'alias': 'Oscar Petersen'
      }, {
        'sort-name': 'Petterson, Oscar',
        'alias': 'Oscar Petterson'
      }
    ],
    'area': {
      'sort-name': 'Canada',
      'id': '71bbafaa-e825-3e15-8ca9-017dcad1748b',
      'name': 'Canada'
    },
    'type': 'Person',
    'name': 'Oscar Peterson'
  },
...
```

This is the default data we get back for Oscar Peterson. It's mostly biodemographic data (someone actually tagged him with `death by kidney failure`), but I'm most interested in the `'ext:score'`, `'id'`, and `'tag-list'` fields. The `'ext:score'` is MB's score of this result's relevance to our query, and `'id'` is the universally unique identifier (UUID) of this record in MB. We'll use `'tag-list'` to try to figure out what instrument an artist plays.

That UUID is known as the MBID ID (MusicBrainz ID), and is used to get more information about an entity in MB, or to apply filters to other searches. For instance, if we wanted to get Oscar Peterson's discography, we could do:

```
>>> mb.browse_releases(artist='ed801bdd-f057-41c0-94fb-76cb5676cd59')
{'release-count': 227, 'release-list': [{'id': '0790458a-58ed-329d-
b979-03b788e98c92', 'text-representation': {'script': 'Latn',
...
```

Yep, 227 for Mr. Peterson. Each "release" (essentially an album) has a group of "recordings" (tracks):

```
>>> mb.browse_recordings(release='eb692ad5-0f9c-34ef-aca2-2fa006ebb4ec')
{'recording-count': 9, 'recording-list': [{'id': '0b718b11-318e-43d3-
a831-d38802f76d91', 'length': '312240', 'title': 'I Hear Music'},
...
```

… and we can get the personnel on each track by passing `'artists'` to the includes argument:

```
>>> mb.get_recording_by_id('0b718b11-318e-43d3-a831-d38802f76d91',
includes=['artists'])
{'recording': {'id': '0b718b11-318e-43d3-a831-d38802f76d91',
'length': '312240', 'title': 'I Hear Music', 'artist-credit-phrase':
'Ella Fitzgerald & Oscar Peterson', 'artist-credit': [{'artist':
{'id': '54799c0e-eb45-4eea-996d-c4d71a63c499', 'name': 'Ella
Fitzgerald', 'sort-name': 'Fitzgerald, Ella'}}, ' & ', {'artist':
{'id': 'ed801bdd-f057-41c0-94fb-76cb5676cd59', 'name': 'Oscar
Peterson', 'sort-name': 'Peterson, Oscar'}}]}}
```

Notice that the dictionaries in the `'artist-credit'` list include MBIDs, and that Oscar Peterson's matches the one we used to get his discography. If we wanted, we could now go down the same path with `Ella Fitzgerald`.

Using the API in our application

So how shall we use this fount of jazz recording knowledge? We need almost all of the information it provides, so we should store a local copy. Luckily we've already got a number of models that map nicely to these MB entities. Here's our strategy:

1. If a user search at JMAD returns insufficient results, use the `musicbrainzngs` library to query MB

2. Use the highest scoring results from MB to create the corresponding model instances at JMAD, and provide links to their pages

3. When the user clicks one of those links, query MB for the child objects (an artist's discography, an album's tracks, and so on) and create the corresponding model instances in JMAD

With this pattern, we'll ensure that we're providing up-to-date and accurate information while keeping the app snappy and not hogging too much of the API.

Mocking – when and why

To get the search result that we're asking for in the new functional test without adding it to the database, we're going to extend the search view to do a `search_artists()` at MB. That's exactly the kind of external integration that we should mock out in our test.

A mock is simply a replacement for an object or function in the context of a single test. There are several reasons you might want to mock out external (or even internal) code, particularly in unit tests:

- Mocks improve test isolation

  If our unit test is dependent on an external system working, doesn't that mean our test is not testing a single *unit*? And if the external system fails, is it really fair to fail the test of our code? A mock guarantees that we get the response we need from the outside code, or if need be, the API error we need to handle.

- External calls slow tests down

  We already know that a hallmark of a good test suite is the speed at which it runs. Calls out over the Internet can add hundreds of milliseconds to a single unit test. Mocking takes care of the latency.

- Mocks help us adhere to API rate limits

  Most Internet APIs enforce some type of threshold or rate limiting. In our case, MB asks that we not hit the API anymore than once a second. Mocks help us play nice with our API providers by not sending out bot-like blasts of calls with no end-user benefit.

- We can test for graceful failover

  What do we do if the API returns something we don't expect, like a 404 Not Found or 500 Internal Server Error? We'd probably need a way to handle the error case. But how would we write a test for that if we were using the API directly? Mocks let us return *whatever* response for an external system, including any errors we might want to test.

Adding the MB API to search

Let's add a new test to `IndexViewTestCase` in `solos/tests/test_views.py` for the MB-enabled search. We won't worry about the mock just yet:

```
def test_index_view_returns_external_tracks(self):
    """
    Test that the index view will return artists from the
    MusicBrainz API if none are returned from our database
    """
    response = self.client.get('/', {
        'instrument': 'Bass',
        'artist': 'Jaco Pastorius' # not currently in the DB
    })

    solos = response.context['solos']
    self.assertEqual(len(solos), 1)
    self.assertEqual(solos[0].artist, 'Jaco Pastorius')
```

Run this test, and we'll hit an `AssertionError` when we test the length of the solos context variable. Let's naively add a call to MB in our view at this point to populate that variable, and drop in a debugger to see what it does. Start by importing the `musicbrainzngs` library and setting the user agent for our call:

```
import musicbrainzngs as mb
...
mb.set_useragent('JMAD - http://jmad.us/', version='0.0.1')
```

Then, inside `index`, start at the `if request.GET.get('artist', None):` line and replace it and the rest of the function with the code here, starting at `artist_kwarg`:

def index(request):

```
    ...
    artist_kwarg = request.GET.get('artist', None)
    if artist_kwarg:
        solos_queryset = solos_queryset.\
            filter(artist=artist_kwarg)

    context = {
        'solos': solos_queryset,
    }

    if context['solos'].count() == 0 and artist_kwarg:
        context['solos'] = mb.search_artists(artist_kwarg)

    import pdb;pdb.set_trace()

    return render_to_response('solos/index.html', context)
```

We've imported the MB Python connector, set the user agent string, factored out the artist search term into its own variable, and searched for that artist if our QuerySet has zero results. When we run the test now, the debugger stops just after the `search_artists()` call, so we can see the value of the solos variable:

```
$ python manage.py test solos.tests.test_views.IndexViewTestCase.test_
index_view_returns_exte
rnal_tracks

...
> /Users/kevin/dev/jmad-project/jmad/solos/views.py(27)index()
-> context = {
(Pdb) solos
{'artist-count': 24, 'artist-list': [{'gender': 'male', 'begin-area':
{'id': '0b345109-5a24-4e47-8bc5-44227f0bdcc3', 'sort-name':
'Norristown', 'name': 'Norristown'}, 'sort-name': 'Pastorius,
Jaco'...
```

That's the raw response from the MB API, which we'll need to parse. Hit c to finish out the test (it ends with an `AssertionError` due to solos being of the wrong type).

Encapsulating the API call

In order to keep our code organized, I'd like to put the code for getting tracks from MB in a class method on the `Track` model. Update the view to use an as-yet-nonexistent class method by removing the `musicbrainzngs` import and `mb.set_useragent()` lines, and changing the `search_artists()` line to:

```
context['solos'] = Solo.\
    get_artist_tracks_from_musicbrainz(artist_kwarg)
```

Now running the test tells us, as we knew, that `Solo` does have the method we just called. Let's add it in `solos/models.py`:

```
class Solo(models.Model):
    ...
    @classmethod
    def get_artist_tracks_from_musicbrainz(cls):
        pass
```

Run the tests, and we get `TypeError: get_artist_tracks_from_musicbrainz()` `takes 1 positional argument but 2 were given`. Add an `artist` keyword argument:

```
def get_artist_tracks_from_musicbrainz(cls, artist):
    pass
```

Now running the test hits the break point in our view. Hit c to go through it (and remove it at your earliest convenience), and you'll see a new error `TypeError:` `object of type 'NoneType' has no len()`. Let's have our new method return a blank dictionary for now.

```
def get_artist_tracks_from_musicbrainz(cls, artist):
    return {}
```

Our test now gets us back to `AssertionError: 0 != 1`. It's just one more hop back to where we were. Let's use the MB library here:

```
...
import musicbrainzngs as mb
...
mb.set_useragent('JMAD - http://jmad.us/', version='0.0.1')
...
@classmethod
    def get_artist_tracks_from_musicbrainz(cls, artist):
        return mb.search_artists(artist)
```

Finally, we're back at `AssertionError: 2 != 1`, and if you added the break point back in and checked solos in the view, you'd see it's the raw response from MB. We're ready to move on to test that new class method directly.

Our first mock

We're just beginning to get into the meat of our MusicBrainz integration, and it's finally time to mock out the `search_artists()` call we've been running over and over again. We'll get started with a new test method in `solos/tests/test_models.py`. We'll use the `@patch` decorator, which we'll talk about in just a second:

```python
from unittest.mock import patch
...
    @patch('musicbrainzngs.search_artists')
    def test_get_artist_tracks_from_musicbrainz(
        self,
        mock_mb_search_artists
    ):
        """
        Test that we can make Solos from the MusicBrainz API
        """
        created_solos = Solo.\
            get_artist_tracks_from_musicbrainz(
                'Jaco Pastorius'
            )

        mock_mb_search_artists.assert_called_with(
            'Jaco Pastorius')
        self.assertEqual(len(created_solos), 2)
        self.assertEqual(created_solos[0].artist,
                        'Jaco Pastorius')
        self.assertEqual(created_solos[1].track.name,
                        'Donna Lee')
```

`@patch` is a wonderful little decorator that replaces whatever you'd like with a Python `MagicMock` object. Pass it a string of the dotted path to the object, function, or method you'd like to replace, and `@patch` will replace it with an object with some pretty neat features:

- You can call *any method* on a `MagicMock` object, and it will log that the method was called and go on its merry way
- You can add specific responses to the object if you need it to behave in a certain way for your test

- It will respond sensibly to things like `len()`, `__str__()`, etc
- The `MagicMock` object is made available to you as a variable by an argument passed to your test method

You can read more about `@patch`, `MagicMock`, and the test of `unittest.mock` in the Python documentation at `https://docs.python.org/3.4/library/unittest.mock.html`.

In our example, we're asking `patch` to mock `musicbrainzngs.search_artist`. We add a second argument, `mock_mb_search_results`, to the test method, which puts a reference to the mock object inside our function. Now any calls to `search_artist` will be completely under our control. The original object, function, or method won't do anything it would normally do (like sending requests out over the Internet) without our telling it to do so.

Conveniently, mock objects keep track of whether or not they have been called. In our test method, we're using the mock's `assert_called_with()` method to test that the function being mocked (`search_artists`) was in fact called in the course of the test, and that it was called with a specific argument (`'Jaco Pastorius'`).

Go ahead and run this this test:

```
$ python manage.py test solos.tests.test_models.SoloModelTestCase.test_
get_artist_tracks_from
_musicbrainz

Creating test database for alias 'default'...

F

======================================================================
FAIL: test_get_artist_tracks_from_musicbrainz
(solos.tests.test_models.SoloModelTestCase)
----------------------------------------------------------------------
Traceback (most recent call last):
  File "/usr/local/Cellar/python3/3.4.2_1/Frameworks/Python.framework/
Versio
ns/3.4/lib/python3.4/unittest/mock.py", line 1136, in patched
    return func(*args, **keywargs)
  File "/Users/kevin/dev/jmad-
project/jmad/solos/tests/test_models.py", line 61, in
test_get_artist_tracks_from_musicbrainz
    self.assertEqual(len(created_solos), 2)
AssertionError: 0 != 2
```

```
------------------------------------------------------------
Ran 1 test in 0.003s
```

```
FAILED (failures=1)
Destroying test database for alias 'default'...
```

Since we called `search_artists` in our function, we made it all the way down to testing the length of the function's return value with `assert_called_with` passing. The `len` test fails because by default `MagicMock` returns a `len` of `0`.

Hacking what's returned from a mocked method

Since we've stopped `search_artists` from doing its real work, now we need to teach our test suite to fake a response for it. We'll do this by setting `return_value` of `mock_mb_search_artists` inside our test. Let's hit the MB API directly in the terminal to see how it will respond to our query:

```
>>> mb.search_artists('Jaco Pastorius')
{'artist-list': [{'gender': 'male', 'area': {'id': '489ce91b-6658-
3307-9877-795b68554c98', 'sort-name': 'United States', 'name':
'United States'}, 'country': 'US', 'tag-list': [{'count': '1',
'name': ...
```

We'll need to set a similarly structured dictionary to be the return value of the mock object. Look back earlier in the chapter for the full pretty-printed version of the dictionary. For our purposes, we're only going to respond with the keys and values we need, specifically an `artist-list` list consisting of a single dictionary with keys `name`, `ext:score`, `id`, and `tag-list`. Add the following to the top of `test_get_artist_tracks_from_musicbrainz`:

```
    ...
    mock_mb_search_artists.return_value = {
        'artist-list': [
            {
                'name': 'Jaco Pastorius',
                'ext:score': '100',
                'id': '46a6fac0-2e14-4214-b08e-3bdb1cffa5aa',
                'tag-list': [
                    {
                        'count': '1',
                        'name': 'jazz fusion'
                    },
```

```
                        {
                            'count': '1',
                            'name': 'bassist'
                        }
                    ]
                }
            ]
        }
    ...
```

Now when we run the tests, we get to the same line, but the output changes to `AssertionError: 1 != 2`. This makes sense, since we're currently returning the result of `search_artists`, and we've set the result of that call to a `dict` with one key/value pair. But that's not exactly what we want. What we really want is a `QuerySet` of `Solos` that we can drop right into our existing view and template. For that, we'll need the artist's discography, as well as the track listing for each record.

Taking another look at the `musicbrainzngs` documentation, it looks like `browse_releases` might be of some help, especially if we add `'recordings'` to the includes argument. Let's give it a go:

```
>>> mb.browse_releases(artist='46a6fac0-2e14-4214-b08e-3bdb1cffa5aa',
includes=['recordings'])
```

```
{'release-list': [{'country': 'US', 'release-event-count': 1, 'date':
'1986', 'cover-art-archive': {'count': '0', 'front': 'false',
'artwork': 'false', 'back': 'false'}, 'title': 'PDB', 'medium-count':
1, 'text-representation': {'script': 'Latn', 'language': 'eng'},
'id': '07ae48b5-8ebe-4453-86db-9c45d602c3fe', 'quality': 'normal',
'release-event-list': [{'area': {'id': '489ce91b-6658-3307-9877-
795b68554c98', 'iso-3166-1-code-list': ['US'], 'sort-name': 'United
States', 'name': 'United States'}, 'date': '1986'}], 'medium-list':
[{'position': '1', 'track-list': [{'length': '582826', 'recording':
{'id': 'db029dd5-...
```

It's tough to read the one-liner output, so try it in your own terminal by setting the call to a variable and rendering the output with the `pprint` module. The response is a dictionary of releases by the artist, including a track listing for each release. So in one call we can get all the information we need for a given artist. Let's start incorporating this function by adding it as another patch:

```
@patch('musicbrainzngs.browse_releases')
@patch('musicbrainzngs.search_artists')
def test_get_artist_tracks_from_musicbrainz(
    self,
    mock_mb_search_artists,
    mock_mb_browse_releases
```

```python
    ):
        """
        Test that we can make Solos from the MusicBrainz API
        """
        # set the return value of the mocked search_artists call
        mock_mb_search_artists.return_value = {
            'artist-list': [
                ...
            ]
        }


        # setting a couple recordings to avoid too much nesting
        recording1 = {
            'recording': {
                'id': '12348765-4321-1234-3421-876543210921',
                'title': 'Donna Lee',
            },
            'position': '1'
        }


        recording2 = {
            'recording': {
                'id': '15263748-4321-8765-8765-102938475610',
                'title': 'Sophisticated Lady',
            },
            'position': '6'
        }


        # set the return value of the mocked browse_releases call
        mock_mb_browse_releases.return_value = {
            'release-list': [
                {
                    'title': 'Jaco Pastorius',
                    'id': '876543212-4321-4321-4321-21987654321',
                    'medium-list': [
                        {
                            # see above
                            'track-list': [recording1]
                        }
                    ]
                },
                {
                    'title': 'Invitation',
                    'id': '43215678-5678-4321-1234-901287651234',
```

```
                  'medium-list': [
                      {
                          # see above
                          'track-list': [recording2]
                      }
                  ]
              }
          ]
      }

      created_solos = Solo.\
          get_artist_tracks_from_musicbrainz('Jaco Pastorius')

      mock_mb_search_artists.assert_called_with(
          'Jaco Pastorius')
      mock_mb_browse_releases.assert_called_with(
          '12345678-1234-1234-1234-123456789012',
          includes=['recordings'])
      self.assertEqual(len(created_solos), 2)
      self.assertEqual(created_solos[0].artist,
                      'Jaco Pastorius')
      self.assertEqual(created_solos[1].track.name,
                      'Donna Lee')
```

A few notes to mention here:

- We've got two patches here. Notice that the *first* patch is the *last* argument to the test method. The patch references are passed in reverse order.

- I started out the `return_value` for `mock_mb_browse_releases` with a full single release, then trimmed back as necessary to get one recording from two different releases. I only want to mock what I need to test my own logic.

- Even if it is a stripped down version, that's a big honkin' response, and doesn't do much for the readability of my code. I'll probably tuck that away somewhere in the `solos.tests` package, particularly if I'm going to need it anywhere else. Tests should read like a story about your code. As it stands, this test reads like a phone book.

- I changed the MBID from the real one that I copied and pasted in from my terminal to an obviously fake one. That way I'm sure that I'm calling (mocked) `browse_releases` with the fake. I want to know if a real API call sneaks in somehow.

Implementing the API calls

The last little bit that we need to fill in our `Solo` model is a way of translating MusicBrainz' tags into instruments. Recall that there's no other information in the `search_artists` call that gives us an artist's instrument directly, only tags like `'bassist'` and `'piano jazz'`. I wrote another class method on `Solo` called `get_instrument_from_musicbrainz_tags` that does a simple translation. Have a peek in the source code if you're curious.

After all that, I can freely muck about in the method. Here's the implementation I came up with:

```
from django.utils.text import slugify
...
from albums.models import Album, Track
...
@classmethod
def get_artist_tracks_from_musicbrainz(cls, artist):
    """
    Create Album, Track, and Solo records for artists we find
    in the MusicBrainz API

    :param artist: an artist's name as a string to search for
    :return: Queryset of Solos
    """
    search_results = mb.search_artists(artist)
    best_result = search_results['artist-list'][0]
    instrument = Solo.\
        get_instrument_from_musicbrainz_tags(
            best_result['tag-list']
        )

    for album_dict in mb.browse_releases(
            best_result['id'],
            includes=['recordings'])['release-list']:

        album = Album.objects.\
            create(name=album_dict['title'],
                   artist=artist,
                   slug=slugify(album_dict['title']))

        for track_dict in album_dict['medium-\
list'][0]['track-list']:
            track = Track.objects.create(
                album=album,
```

```
                    name=track_dict['recording']['title'],
                    track_number=track_dict['position'],
                    slug=slugify(
                        track_dict['recording']['title']))

            Solo.objects.create(
                track=track, artist=artist,
                instrument=instrument,
                slug=slugify(artist))

        return Solo.objects.filter(artist=artist)
```

This method gets the test to pass.

Moving back up the chain

Now that we've got a functioning method, we can apply the same pattern to our view test. But instead of mocking out the `musicbrainszngs` calls, we'll mock out our own method. Just for kicks, let's run the view test right now:

```
$ python manage.py test solos.tests.test_views.IndexViewTestCase.test_
index_view_returns_exte
rnal_tracks

...

self.assertEqual(len(solos), 1)

AssertionError: 192 != 1
```

This test hit the MB API directly, and we wound up creating 192 `Solos`, 192 `Tracks`, and a handful of `Albums`. Let's add in the mock:

```
    from unittest.mock import patch, Mock
    ...
        @patch('solos.models.Solo.get_artist_tracks_from_musicbrainz')
        def test_index_view_returns_external_tracks(
            self,
            mock_solos_get_from_mb
        ):
            """
            Test that the index view will return artists from the
            MusicBrainz API if none are returned from our
            database
            """
            mock_solo = Mock()
            mock_solo.artist = 'Jaco Pastorius'
            mock_solos_get_from_mb.return_value = [mock_solo]
```

```
response = self.client.get('/', {
    'instrument': 'Bass',
    'artist': 'Jaco Pastorius' # not in our DB
})

solos = response.context['solos']
self.assertEqual(len(solos), 1)
self.assertEqual(solos[0].artist, 'Jaco Pastorius')
```

We're doing two mocks here. We mock the call to get_artist_tracks_from_ musicbrainz and create a mocked Solo with a unittest.mock.Mock object (have a look at the Python docs for details). We then return the mock object in the list we set as return_value for out mocked method. This gets our test to pass:

```
$ python manage.py test solos.tests.test_views.IndexViewTestCase.test_
index_view_returns_exte
rnal_tracks
Creating test database for alias 'default'...

.
-----------------------------------------------------------------

Ran 1 test in 0.009s


OK
Destroying test database for alias 'default'...


Give the full test suite a run.
$ python manage.py test
Creating test database for alias 'default'...

.............
-----------------------------------------------------------------
Ran 13 tests in 17.090s


OK
```

Now we can commit. Notice that we didn't commit at any point during this chapter (save for the tags method not listed here). Since we had test code hitting the live MB API, I didn't feel we were ready to call the code anything like done. Now we're ready.

```
$ git commit -am 'Integrates MusicBrainzNGS API'
$ git tag -a ch6-1-integrate-mb
```

Dealing with change

Our application is now dependent upon an outside resource for part of its functionality. What happens when the MusicBrainz API changes, breaking our application but leaving our tests passing? In this example, we'd have to go back through and update the dictionary responses to match the changes in MusicBrainz. No fun.

Tools such as VCR.py (https://github.com/kevin1024/vcrpy) can help here. VCR.py will record HTTP responses in YAML files during an initial test run, then each subsequent test run will use the recorded version instead of making a new call. Then, if the API changes, just delete the recorded versions to get a fresh copy (and some broken tests to fix).

This is just one method

There are lots of ways to integrate with third-party APIs, and still more ways of testing those integrations. In this case we happened to have access to an existing Python library that abstracts away the actual HTTP requests. We won't always have that luxury.

When faced with a REST API integration to build from scratch, I recommend the superb requests library (http://docs.python-requests.org/). It makes the process of interacting with HTTP as beautiful as Python itself. Then mock the responses with VCR.py or Betamax (http://betamax.readthedocs.org/) a tool similar to VCR.py but built specifically to work with requests.

Summary

In this chapter, we looked at a few reasons why we might want to add mocks to our tests. We learned a bit about patch and Mock from unittest.mock, as well as how to write tests when using an external API.

In the next chapter, we'll turn this chapter inside out, building an API for other systems to interact with our application.

7
Share and Share Alike

In this chapter, we'll expose the data in our application via a REST API. As we do, we'll learn:

- The importance of documentation in the API development process
- How to write functional tests for API endpoints
- API patterns and best practices

It's an API world, we're just coding in it

It's very common nowadays to include a public REST API in your web project. Exposing your services or data to the world is generally done for one of two reasons:

- You've got interesting data, and other developers might want to integrate that information into a project they're working on
- You're building a secondary system that you expect your users to interact with, and that system needs to interact with your data (that is, a mobile or desktop app, or an AJAX-driven front end)

We've got both reasons in our application. We're housing novel, interesting data in our database that someone might want to access programmatically. Also, it would make sense to build a desktop application that could interact with a user's own digital music collection so they could actually hear the solos we're storing in our system.

Deceptive simplicity

The good news is that there are some great options for third-party plugins for Django that allow you to build a REST API into an existing application. The bad news is that the simplicity of adding one of these packages can let you go off half-cocked, throwing an API on top of your project without a real plan for it.

If you're lucky, you'll just wind up with a bird's nest of an API: inconsistent URLs, wildly varying payloads, and difficult authentication. In the worst-case scenario, your bolt-on API exposes data you didn't intend to make public and you wind up with a self-inflicted security issue.

Never forget that an API is sort of invisible. Unlike traditional web pages, where bugs are very public and easy to describe, API bugs are only visible to other developers. Take special care to make sure your API behaves exactly as intended by writing thorough documentation and tests to make sure you've implemented it correctly.

Writing documentation first

"*Documentation is king.*"

- *Kenneth Reitz*

If you've spent any time at all working with Python or Django, you know what good documentation looks like. The Django folks in particular seem to understand this well: the key to getting developers to use your code is great documentation.

In documenting an API, be explicit. Most of your API methods' docs should take the form of "if you send this, you will get back this," with real-world examples of input and output.

A great side effect of prewriting documentation is that it makes the intention of your API crystal clear. You're allowing yourself to conjure up the API from thin air without getting bogged down in any of the details, so you can get a bird's-eye view of what you're trying to accomplish. Your documentation will keep you oriented throughout the development process.

Documentation-Driven testing

Once you've got your documentation done, testing is simply a matter of writing test cases that match up with what you've promised. The actions of the test methods exercise HTTP methods, and your assertions check the responses.

Test-Driven Development really shines when it comes to API development. There are great tools for sending JSON over the wire, but properly formatting JSON can be a pain, and reading it can be worse. Enshrining test JSON in test methods and asserting they match the real responses will save you a ton of headache.

More developers, more problems

Good documentation and test coverage are exponentially more important when two groups are developing in tandem—one on the client application and one on the API. Changes to an API are hard for teams like this to deal with, and should come with a lot of warning (and apologies). If you have to make a change to an endpoint, it *should* break a lot of tests, and you should methodically go and fix them all. What's more, no one feels the pain of regression bugs like the developer of an API-consuming client. You really, really, *really* need to know that all the endpoints you've put out there are still going to work when you add features or refactor.

Building an API with Django REST framework

Now that you're properly terrified of developing an API, let's get started. What sort of capabilities should we add? Here are a couple possibilities:

- Exposing the `Album`, `Track`, and `Solo` information we have
- Creating new `Solos` or updating existing ones

Initial documentation

In the Python world it's very common for documentation to live in docstrings, as it keeps the description of how to use an object close to the implementation. We'll eventually do the same with our docs, but it's kind of hard to write a docstring for a method that doesn't exist yet. Let's open up a new Markdown file `API.md`, right in the root of the project, just to get us started. If you've never used Markdown before, you can read an introduction to GitHub's version of Markdown at `https://help.github.com/articles/markdown-basics/`.

Here's a sample of what should go in `API.md`. Have a look at `https://github.com/kevinharvey/jmad/blob/master/API.md` for the full, rendered version.

```
...
# Get a Track with Solos

 * URL: /api/tracks/\<pk\>/
 * HTTP Method: GET

## Example Response

    {
        "name": "All Blues",
        "slug": "all-blues",
        "album": {
```

```
            "name": "Kind of Blue",
            "url": "http://jmad.us/api/albums/2/"
        },
        "solos": [
            {
                "artist": "Cannonball Adderley",
                "instrument": "saxophone",
                "start_time": "4:05",
                "end_time": "6:04",
                "slug": "cannonball-adderley",
                "url": "http://jmad.us/api/solos/281/"
            },
            ...
        ]
    }
```

Add a Solo to a Track

 * URL: /api/solos/
 * HTTP Method: POST

Example Request

```
    {
        "track": "/api/tracks/83/",
        "artist": "Don Cherry",
        "instrument": "cornet",
        "start_time": "2:13",
        "end_time": "3:54"
    }
```

Example Response

```
    {
        "url": "http://jmad.us/api/solos/64/",
        "artist": "Don Cherry",
        "slug": "don-cherry",
        "instrument": "cornet",
        "start_time": "2:13",
        "end_time": "3:54",
        "track": "http://jmad.us/api/tracks/83/"
    }
```

There's not a lot of prose, and there needn't be. All we're trying to do is layout the ins and outs of our API. It's important at this point to step back and have a look at the endpoints in their totality. Is there enough of a pattern that you can sort of guess what the next one is going to look like? Does it look like a fairly straightforward API to interact with? Does anything about it feel clunky? Would you want to work with this API yourself? Take time to think through any weirdness now before anything gets out in the wild.

```
$ git commit -am 'Initial API Documentation'
$ git tag -a ch7-1-init-api-docs
```

Introducing Django REST framework

Now that we've got some idea what we're building, let's actually get it going. We'll be using Django REST Framework (http://www.django-rest-framework.org/). Start by installing it in your environment:

```
$ pip install djangorestframework
```

Add rest_framework to your INSTALLED_APPS in jmad/settings.py:

```
INSTALLED_APPS = (
    ...
    'rest_framework'
)
```

Now we're ready to start testing.

Writing tests for API endpoints

While there's no such thing as browser-based testing for an external API, it is important to write tests that cover its end-to-end processing. We need to be able to send in requests like the ones we've documented and confirm that we receive the responses our documentation promises.

Django REST Framework (DRF from here on out) provides tools to help write tests for the application functionality it provides. We'll use rest_framework.tests. APITestCase to write functional tests. Let's kick off with the list of albums. Convert albums/tests.py to a package, and add a test_api.py file. Then add the following:

```
from rest_framework.test import APITestCase

from albums.models import Album
```

```
class AlbumAPITestCase(APITestCase):

    def setUp(self):
        self.kind_of_blue = Album.objects.create(
                              name='Kind of Blue')
        self.a_love_supreme = Album.objects.create(
                              name='A Love Supreme')


    def test_list_albums(self):
        """
        Test that we can get a list of albums
        """
        response = self.client.get('/api/albums/')

        self.assertEqual(response.status_code, 200)
        self.assertEqual(response.data[0]['name'],
                    'A Love Supreme')
        self.assertEqual(response.data[1]['url'],
                    'http://testserver/api/albums/1/')
```

Since much of this is very similar to other tests that we've seen before, let's talk about the important differences:

- We import and subclass APITestCase, which makes self.client an instance of rest_framework.test.APIClient. Both of these subclass their respective django.test counterparts add a few niceties that help in testing APIs (none of which are showcased yet).

- We test response.data, which we expect to be a list of Albums. response.data will be a Python dict or list that corresponds to the JSON payload of the response.

- During the course of the test, APIClient (a subclass of Client) will use http://testserver as the protocol and hostname for the server, and our API should return a host-specific URI.

Run this test, and we get the following:

```
$ python manage.py test albums.tests.test_api
Creating test database for alias 'default'...
F

======================================================================
FAIL: test_list_albums (albums.tests.test_api.AlbumAPITestCase)
Test that we can get a list of albums
```

```
Traceback (most recent call last):
  File "/Users/kevin/dev/jmad-project/jmad/albums/tests/test_api.py",
line 17, in test_list_albums
    self.assertEqual(response.status_code, 200)
AssertionError: 404 != 200
```

```
Ran 1 test in 0.019s
```

FAILED (failures=1)

We're failing because we're getting a 404 Not Found instead of a 200 OK status code. Proper HTTP communication is important in any web application, but it really comes in to play when you're using AJAX. Most frontend libraries will properly classify responses as successful or erroneous based on the status code: making sure the code are on point will save your frontend developers friends a lot of headache.

We're getting a 404 because we don't have a URL defined yet. Before we set up the route, let's add a quick unit test for routing. Update the test case with one new import and method:

```python
from django.core.urlresolvers import resolve
...
    def test_album_list_route(self):
        """
        Test that we've got routing set up for Albums
        """
        route = resolve('/api/albums/')

        self.assertEqual(route.func.__name__, 'AlbumViewSet')
```

Here, we're just confirming that the URL routes to the correct view. Run it:

```
$ python manage.py test
albums.tests.test_api.AlbumAPITestCase.test_album_list_route
...
django.core.urlresolvers.Resolver404: {'path': 'api/albums/',
'tried': [[<RegexURLResolver <RegexURLPattern list> (admin:admin)
^admin/>], [<RegexURLPattern solo_detail_view
^recordings/(?P<album>[\w-]+)/(?P<track>[\w-]+)/(?P<artist>[\w-
]+)/$>], [<RegexURLPattern None ^$>]]}
```

```
-----------------------------------------------------------------
Ran 1 test in 0.003s
```

```
FAILED (errors=1)
```

We get a `Resolver404` error, which is expected since Django shouldn't return anything at that path. Now we're ready to set up our URLs.

API routing with DRF's SimpleRouter

Take a look at the documentation for routers at `http://www.django-rest -framework.org/api-guide/routers/`. They're a very clean way of setting up URLs for DRF-powered views. Update `jmad/urls.py` like so:

```python
...
from rest_framework import routers

from albums.views import AlbumViewSet


router = routers.SimpleRouter()
router.register(r'albums', AlbumViewSet)

urlpatterns = [

    # Admin
    url(r'^admin/', include(admin.site.urls)),

    # API
    url(r'^api/', include(router.urls)),

    # Apps
    url(r'^recordings/(?P<album>[\w-]+)/(?P<track>[\w-]+)/
(?P<artist>[\w-]+)/$',
        'solos.views.solo_detail',
        name='solo_detail_view'),
    url(r'^$', 'solos.views.index'),
]
```

Here's what we changed:

- We created an instance of `SimpleRouter` and used the `register` method to set up a route. The `register` method has two required arguments: a `prefix` to build the route methods from, and something called a `viewset`. Here we've supplied a non-existent class `AlbumViewSet`, which we'll come back to later.

- We've added a few comments to break up our `urls.py`, which was starting to look a little like a rat's nest.

- The actual API URLs are registered under the `'^api/'` path using Django's `include` function.

Run the URL test again, and we'll get `ImportError` for `AlbumViewSet`. Let's add a stub to `albums/views.py`:

```
class AlbumViewSet():
    pass
```

Run the test now, and we'll start to see some specific DRF error messages to help us build out our view:

```
$ python manage.py test
albums.tests.test_api.AlbumAPITestCase.test_album_list_route

Creating test database for alias 'default'...

F

...

  File "/Users/kevin/.virtualenvs/jmad/lib/python3.4/site-
packages/rest_framework/routers.py", line 60, in register

    base_name = self.get_default_base_name(viewset)

  File "/Users/kevin/.virtualenvs/jmad/lib/python3.4/site-
packages/rest_framework/routers.py", line 135, in
get_default_base_name

    assert queryset is not None, ''base_name' argument not specified,
and could ' \

AssertionError: 'base_name' argument not specified, and could not
automatically determine the name from the viewset, as it does not
have a '.queryset' attribute.
```

After a fairly lengthy output, the test runner tells us that it was unable to get `base_name` for the URL, as we did not specify the `base_name` in the `register` method, and it couldn't guess the name because the viewset (`AlbumViewSet`) did not have a `queryset` attribute.

In the router documentation, we came across the optional `base_name` argument for register (as well as the exact wording of this error). You can use that argument to control the name your URL gets. However, let's keep letting DRF do its default behavior. We haven't read the documentation for viewsets yet, but we know that a regular Django class-based view expects a `queryset` parameter. Let's stick one on `AlbumViewSet` and see what happens:

```
from .models import Album


class AlbumViewSet():
    queryset = Album.objects.all()
```

Run the test again, and we get:

```
django.core.urlresolvers.Resolver404: {'path': 'api/albums/',
'tried': [[<RegexURLResolver <RegexURLPattern list> (admin:admin)
^admin/>], [<RegexURLPattern solo_detail_view
^recordings/(?P<album>[\w-]+)/(?P<track>[\w-]+)/(?P<artist>[\w-
]+)/$>], [<RegexURLPattern None ^$>]]}


----------------------------------------------------------------

Ran 1 test in 0.011s


FAILED (errors=1)
```

Huh? Another `404` is a step backwards. What did we do wrong? Maybe it's time to figure out what a viewset really is.

Automatic APIs with DRF viewsets

Viewsets are DRF's way of handling one or more of the various HTTP verbs (GET, POST, PUT, PATCH, DELETE, HEAD, and OPTIONS) for a given resource with a single view class. They take into account two types of API actions: those performed on a single object, and those performed on a list of objects. Viewsets handle these types of actions and the verbs that do them with specific methods on the class.

This all sounds a little confusing, but what it really means is that to allow an action through a viewset, you've got to add that action's method to the viewset class. Once the method is there, the router will automatically set up the URL to support it, and route incoming requests with the corresponding HTTP verb to that method.

Here's a table of what's available, using our `Album` example:

Action to perform	URL	HTTP verb	The method that we should provide
Get a list of objects	`/api/albums/`	GET	`list()`
Create a new object	`/api/albums/`	POST	`create()`
Get an instance of an object	`/api/albums/<pk>/`	GET	`retrieve()`
Update an object	`/api/albums/<pk>/`	PUT	`update()`
Update an object (with partial fields)	`/api/albums/<pk>/`	PATCH	`partial_ update()`
Delete an object	`/api/albums/<pk>/`	DELETE	`destroy()`

Have a look at the documentation to get the full story: `http://www.django-rest -framework.org/api-guide/viewsets/`.

For now, let's try to fix this `404` error by adding a `list()` method:

```
...
class AlbumViewSet():
    queryset = Album.objects.all()

    def list(self):
        pass
```

Now our test tells us `AttributeError: type object 'AlbumViewSet' has no attribute 'as_view'`. We need to subclass DRF's `GenericViewset`, which not only provides the `as_view` method, but also `get_object` and `get_queryset`, which hook into a lot of the DRF machinery that handle permissions and authentication:

```
from rest_framework import viewsets
...
class AlbumViewSet(viewsets.GenericViewSet):
...
```

Run the test, and it passes! How about the functional test?

```
$ python manage.py test
albums.tests.test_api.AlbumAPITestCase.test_list_albums

...

TypeError: list() takes 1 positional argument but 2 were given
```

Easy enough, our method needs to accept the request as an argument. However, instead of fixing up our list method, let's try using DRF's ListModelMixin (which provides a list method, http://www.django-rest-framework.org/api-guide/generic-views/#listmodelmixin). Remove our list method, and add the mixin to the class declaration. albums/views.py file should now look like this:

```
from rest_framework import viewsets, mixins

from .models import Album


class AlbumViewSet(viewsets.GenericViewSet,
                   mixins.ListModelMixin):
    queryset = Album.objects.all()
```

How does our functional test look now?

```
$ python manage.py test
albums.tests.test_api.AlbumAPITestCase.test_list_albums

...

AssertionError: 'AlbumViewSet' should either include a
'serializer_class' attribute, or override the
'get_serializer_class()' method.
```

This error prompts us to implement one of the most powerful features of DRF—a model serializer.

Converting Django models with serializers

Serializers do the heavy lifting when it comes to creating JSON representations from Django QuerySets, and vice versa. We'll use them to define what fields we want to expose on a model, and perform any validation on data coming into the API. There's tons of power available in DRF's serializer classes, much of which we won't need for this first simple endpoint.

First things first, let's fix AssertionError by adding the following attribute:

```
from .serializers import AlbumSerializer
...
class AlbumViewSet(viewsets.GenericViewSet, mixins.ListModelMixin):
    ...
    serializer_class = AlbumSerializer
```

That'll land us `ImportError` when we run the test, so create `albums/serializers.py` and add in the following:

```
class AlbumSerializer():
    pass
```

Run the tests now, and we see that our stubbed `AlbumSerializer` needs some more functionality:

```
$ python manage.py test
...
  File "/Users/kevin/.virtualenvs/jmad/lib/python3.4/site-
packages/rest_framework/generics.py", line 109, in get_serializer
    return serializer_class(*args, **kwargs)
TypeError: object() takes no parameters
```

It's time to pick one of DRF's serializer classes to subclass from. Since our documentation calls for a 'url' field to be returned for each album (it's best practice to return the URI for an object whenever possible), let's use `HyperlinkedModelSerializer`:

```
from rest_framework import serializers

from .models import Album


class AlbumSerializer(
        serializers.HyperlinkedModelSerializer):
    class Meta:
        model = Album
```

Read up on serializers at `http://www.django-rest-framework.org/api-guide/serializers/`. `HyperlinkedModelSerializer` comes with lots of goodies, and all we have to do to get them is pass our model to the subclass' `Meta`.

Warning

`HyperlinkModelSerializer` provides `create()` and `update()` methods for the Album model. However, since we didn't add `CreateModelMixin` or `UpdateModelMixin` to the viewset, they aren't exposed via the API. Note that it would take a very small change to do so (either add the mixins, or the subclass `ModelViewSet` instead of `GenericViewSet`). DRF gives you a lot of stuff for free, but always make sure that you really want what it's providing, particularly when you're using more full-featured classes.

Finishing up with RetrieveModelMixin

Now, our test gives us a very helpful error:

```
$ python manage.py test albums.tests.test_api.AlbumAPITestCase.test_list_
albums

Creating test database for alias 'default'...

E

=====================================================================

ERROR: test_list_albums (albums.tests.test_api.AlbumAPITestCase)

Test that we can get a list of albums

---------------------------------------------------------------------

...

(lookup_view_s, args, kwargs, len(patterns), patterns))

django.core.urlresolvers.NoReverseMatch: Reverse for 'album-detail'
with arguments '()' and keyword arguments '{'pk': 2}' not found. 0
pattern(s) tried: []


During handling of the above exception, another exception occurred:

...

File "/Users/kevin/.virtualenvs/jmad/lib/python3.4/site-
packages/rest_framework/relations.py", line 272, in to_representation

    raise ImproperlyConfigured(msg % self.view_name)

django.core.exceptions.ImproperlyConfigured: Could not resolve URL
for hyperlinked relationship using view name "album-detail". You may
have failed to include the related model in your API, or incorrectly
configured the 'lookup_field' attribute on this field.
```

Our `HyperlinkedModelSerializer` can't find a URL to provide for an Album
instance. And of course it can't because we haven't provided it yet. All our view will
currently do is list albums. We need to make one change to get a view for single
albums. In `albums/views.py`, add `RetrieveModelMixin` to `AlbumViewSet`:

```
    class AlbumViewSet(viewsets.GenericViewSet,
                       mixins.ListModelMixin,
                       mixins.RetrieveModelMixin):
    ...
```

And now, low and behold, our tests pass:

```
$ python manage.py test albums.tests.test_api.AlbumAPITestCase
Creating test database for alias 'default'...
..
```

```
----------------------------------------------------------------
Ran 2 tests in 0.018s


OK
Destroying test database for alias 'default'...
```

It's worth noting how little unit testing we did to get this endpoint working. Our single functional test was enough to guide us through almost the entire process, most of which was just configuration of subclassed DRF resources. We did not have a lot of custom logic to test.

We did add a stub view method and URL in the course of finishing the list test. The next step would be to build out that view with another functional test, but for now let's commit and move on to adding new `Solo` data via the API.

```
$ git commit -am 'Initial config for DRF, Album list and retrieve'
$ git tag -a ch7-2-init-drf
```

Adding data via the API

In order to get to this point, I've skipped ahead a bit, repeating much of the same work on the `Album` endpoint for `Tracks`. Either take a peak in the repo, or better yet, attempt the following tasks on your own and come back to the source to compare:

1. Write a functional test for listing `Tracks`
2. Add serializers for `Solos` and `Tracks`
3. Write a `TrackViewSet` to satisfy the functional test

If you'd like to grab the code from the repository:

```
$ git checkout ch7-3-track-view-and-serializer
```

Now we're ready to open up our API for new, incoming Solo data.

POSTing data in a test

Let's start by writing a new functional test for adding Solos via the API. We'll use `APIClient.post` to send a `dict` (as JSON) to `'/api/solos/'`. Create a new file `solos/tests/test_api.py` and enter:

```
from rest_framework.test import APITestCase

from albums.models import Album, Track
```

```python
class SoloAPITestCase(APITestCase):

    def setUp(self):
        self.giant_steps = Album.objects.create(
                            name='Giant Steps',
                            slug='giant-steps'
        )
        self.mr_pc = Track.objects.create(
                            name='Mr. PC',
                            slug='mr-pc',
                            album=self.giant_steps
        )


    def test_create_solo(self):
        """
        Test that we can create a solo
        """
        post_data = {
            'track': '/api/tracks/2/',
            'artist': 'John Coltrane',
            'instrument': 'saxophone',
            'start_time': '0:24',
            'end_time': '3:21'
        }
        response = self.client.post('/api/solos/',
                                    data=post_data,
format='json')

        self.assertEqual(response.status_code, 201)
        self.assertEqual(response.data, {
            'url': 'http://testserver/api/solos/1/',
            'artist': 'John Coltrane',
            'slug': 'john-coltrane',
            'instrument': 'saxophone',
            'start_time': '0:24',
            'end_time': '3:21',
            'track': 'http://testserver/api/tracks/1/'
        })
```

In the preceding snippet, note that:

1. We pass three arguments to `self.client.post`: the URL to post to, the data to send, and the 'format', which sets the `Content-Type` header on the request.

2. We're looking for a `201 Created` response, since we are adding new data

Running the test from here, we go through a similar process as in the `AlbumViewSet` build out. Our first failure is a `404 Not Found` status code, where we expected a `201`. Go ahead and build out the view on your own. When I did it, I wrote another test for the URL using `resolve`, and went through the following steps:

1. Update the router with a proposed, then stubbed, `SoloViewSet`.

2. Develop `SoloViewSet` by subclassing `GenericViewSet` and adding a `queryset` and a stubbed `SoloSerializer` as a `serializer_class`.

3. Develop `SoloSerializer` by subclassing `HyperlinkedModelSerializer`, and set its `model Meta` attribute to `Solo`.

4. Add DRF's `CreateModelMixin` to `SoloViewSet` to allow creation via `POST`.

Have a look here if you get stuck:

```
$ git checkout ch7-4-solo-view-and-serializer
```

After all that, I ran my functional test and got:

```
$ python manage.py test solos.tests.test_api.SoloAPITestCase.test_create_
solo
Creating test database for alias 'default'...
F
======================================================================
FAIL: test_create_solo (solos.tests.test_api.SoloAPITestCase)
Test that we can get a list of albums
----------------------------------------------------------------------
Traceback (most recent call last):
  File "/Users/kevin/dev/jmad-project/jmad/solos/tests/test_api.py",
line 25, in test_create_solo
    self.assertEqual(response.status_code, 201)
AssertionError: 400 != 201
```

DRF viewsets return `400 Bad Request` responses when any number of problems occur, often payload validation errors. 400s are generally accompanied by a message in the response payload to describe the error.

Let's add that payload to our status code assertion statement to see what's going on. In `solos/test_api.py`:

```
self.assertEqual(response.status_code, 201, response.data)
```

Now when we run the test, we get:

AssertionError: 400 != 201 : {'slug': ['This field is required.']}

We'd like for slugs to be autogenerated, but they're required fields on our model. Let's take care of this in the serializer.

Validating inbound data with a serializer

Generating a slug from another submitted value is an excellent reason to write a custom validate method on our `SoloSerializer`. `validate` is defined on `Serializer` (which is a little further up the inheritance ladder from `HyperlinkedModelSerializer`) as a pass through, called in all the right places and just waiting to be overwritten by implementers like us. It takes one argument, a `dict` of the data passed to the serializer, and must return a similarly structured `dict`.

We've been basing our slugs off the `'artist'` field on `Solo`, and we know that we're passing an `'artist'` field into the Solo endpoint. Let's write a test to make sure we can slugify the artist field and add it to the data passed through our custom validate class. Here's what I came up with in `solos/tests/test_serializers.py`:

```python
from unittest import TestCase

from solos.serializers import SoloSerializer


class SoloSerializerTestCase(TestCase):

    def test_validate(self):
        """
        Tests that SoloSerializer.validate() adds a slugged
        version of the artist attribute to the data
        """
        serializer = SoloSerializer()
        data = serializer.validate({'artist': 'Ray Brown'})

        self.assertEqual(data, {
            'artist': 'Ray Brown',
            'slug': 'ray-brown'
        })
```

Run the test, and we can see the default pass-through behavior of `validate`:

```
$ python manage.py test solos.tests.test_serializers
Creating test database for alias 'default'...
F
...
AssertionError: {'artist': 'Ray Brown'} != {'artist': 'Ray Brown',
'slug': 'ray-brown'}
- {'artist': 'Ray Brown'}
+ {'artist': 'Ray Brown', 'slug': 'ray-brown'}
```

Let's overwrite validate to provide a slug value. Back in `solos/serializers.py`:

```
from django.utils.text import slugify
...
class SoloSerializer(serializers.HyperlinkedModelSerializer):
    ...
    def validate(self, data):
        data['slug'] = slugify(data['artist'])
        return data
```

This is a very lightweight validate and doesn't take into account an update to an existing instance, but I'm going to save that refactor for when I expose the `update` method sometime in the future. Now this passes the test. Let's run the functional test now:

```
$ python manage.py test solos.tests.test_api.SoloAPITestCase.test_create_
solo
...
AssertionError: 400 != 201 : {'slug': ['This field is required.']}
```

Same error? Oh yeah, `SoloSerializer` is looking for slug right out of the gate, before it even runs `validate` (you can confirm this by dropping a `pdb.set_trace()` in `validate` and running the test again). We want slug to be a read only field. Add the declaration to `SoloSerializer.Meta` in `solos/serializers.py`:

```
class SoloSerializer(serializers.HyperlinkedModelSerializer):
    class Meta:
        model = Solo
        read_only_fields = ('slug',)
    ...
```

Let's try this again:

```
$ python manage.py test solos.tests.test_api.SoloAPITestCase.test_create_
solo
```

```
...
```

```
raise ImproperlyConfigured(msg % self.view_name)
```

```
django.core.exceptions.ImproperlyConfigured: Could not resolve URL
for hyperlinked relationship using view name "solo-detail". You may
have failed to include the related model in your API, or incorrectly
configured the 'lookup_field' attribute on this field.
```

We saw a similar error earlier on `AlbumViewSet`. All we need to do is include the `RetrieveModelMixin`:

```
    ...
    class SoloViewSet(viewsets.GenericViewSet,
                      mixins.CreateModelMixin,
                      mixins.RetrieveModelMixin):
    ...
```

Finally, we passed! Let's run the full suite.

```
$ python manage.py test
Creating test database for alias 'default'...
.................
----------------------------------------------------------------------
Ran 20 tests in 22.708s

OK (skipped=1)
Destroying test database for alias 'default'...
```

And commit:

```
$ git commit -am 'Sets slug field from artist via serializer method'
$ git tag -a ch7-5-slug-in-serializer
```

Summary

In this chapter, we covered basic API design and testing patterns, including the importance of documentation when developing an API. In doing so, we took a deep dive into Django REST Framework and the utilities and testing tools available in it.

Next, we'll take a look back at what we've learned over the last seven chapters and talk about the next steps in your TDD journey.

8
Promises Kept

In this chapter, we will:

- Look back on what we've accomplished through TDD
- Assess what TDD did not cover in our project
- Explore related topics and other development activities to build on the foundation we've created

How far we've come

Over the course of the last seven chapters, we've managed to build:

- A database for storing data about jazz solos
- A user interface for searching and viewing that information
- A connection to an API where we can get source information for jazz artists and albums
- An API for accessing our data via external applications

All the while we've written our tests first, letting the failing tests drive our next steps.

So, how did it go?

Now that you've got a taste of what TDD is about, let's look back at the benefits promised in *Chapter 1, Keeping Your Promises* as well as the common criticisms of TDD, and see how our experience compares.

We kept ourselves on track

We definitely built only what we needed; our project is nothing if not lean and mean. We've got just enough code to cover the handful of user stories that we wanted to address. TDD kept us from building tangential features that we might not ever need. Our code stayed nimble, testable, and ready to be refactored as new user stories come in to play.

Our application can check itself

Every line of code, from model methods to external API interactions, is exercised in a run of our test suite. We'll always know it's working, and we can change it in controlled ways by amending or adding tests before we tinker with the logic.

We kept our thinking clear

Particularly in building our external API, our up-front tests really made us think about what we were trying to accomplish before we started. We captured and quantified the often squishy, "hey-can-you-make-it-do-this" requirements into functional tests, so we know that we finished what we promised our client.

Our code is testable

This is about as self-evident as a benefit can be, but it's worth stating that our entire application is written in a very testable way: it's modular, logical branching is kept to a minimum, and there's very little "magic".

We can take big risks

Want to try replacing SQLite with PostgreSQL? Want to swap out some of those function-based views for their class-based counterparts? Go ahead and make broadly sweeping changes. The test suite we've built along side our application will walk you through any errors that you make in refactoring, and show you exactly where you need to adjust your code to get a new version of the application running.

We look like pros

Our test suite communicates to other developers who may be interested in helping with our project (wink, wink) that we're taking it very seriously. We've followed best practices, and the code that we've written works.

Did we do more work than necessary?

One reason often given for avoiding tests (let alone writing them first) is that it's extra work with little benefit. If you're measuring work by counting the lines of code, we've definitely done more work in this project than if we'd stuck to just cranking out models, views, and templates. But if you value test coverage, there's no way we've exerted more effort than had we tried to write tests after the fact. On the contrary, in many cases, the application code itself was trivial to write after we'd thought it through in the test writing phase.

What we unfortunately did not get to experience is the utter joy of a major refactor with a full-test suite in place. Good test coverage saves us from having to go back and hand-check all the code after we do something like changing a CharField to a ForeignKey. Here I'd argue that the TDD approach outpaces even testless development.

Did it take longer than it should have?

Again, if we're comparing against untested coding, we probably did spend more time on developing in the green field. But if we don't consider our project done until there's a comprehensive test suite in place, TDD will definitely get us there fast. Writing tests first necessarily requires us to ask ourselves "How would I test this?" from the very beginning, hence our code comes out clean and fast. And once again, we'll be paid back that time in spades when we refactor.

What haven't we done?

Our development thus far has focused on basic user experience and the business logic of the application. There are some big holes in what's left to do, some of which TDD can help us with, and some better left to other processes.

Production optimization

We've eschewed any optimization in the interest of keeping our tests running fast. The biggest change to make would be the database backend. We've been using the default SQLite, but we'll likely use PostgreSQL for production. Building a new PostgreSQL database for every run takes a bit more time, so I'll probably continue to run tests locally with SQLite in memory. However, we need to make sure our tests still pass with our production DB in place.

The best solution is likely a combination of dedicated `settings.py` files and some sort of continuous integration (CI) setup. CI means different things to different people, but to me the minimal CI setup can:

- Check out code from repository
- Run the tests
- Inform if it failed

The next step might be for the CI server to actually deploy your code, but we're more interested in getting the tests run. Configure your CI as close to production as possible. A test suite slowed by building a PostgreSQL database may break my flow, but an automated CI server doesn't mind at all how long it takes.

To keep different settings for your production and local instances, I'd recommend the set up described in *Two Scoops of Django* by Daniel Roy Greenfeld and Audrey Roy Greenfeld. A simplified version of this might be as easy as leaving your current settings file in place but adding `prod.py` next to it. Start off with a wholesale import from `settings.py`, only overwriting what you need to change:

```
From jmad.settings import *

DEBUG = False

DATABASES = {
    ...
    # your production DB settings here
}
```

Then configure your CI to run tests with `python manage.py test --settings=jmad.prod`. Similarly your WSGI file would use `prod.py` as its settings file.

An actual frontend design

To put it generously, our current design is very *clean*. We definitely need some thoughtful design work in our templates. Design is not a place where TDD can help us, but our test suite (most importantly the functional test) can let us know if any design elements interfere with the user experience. If substantial changes need to be made, we might need to go back and update the Selenium selectors.

Quality assurance

I can hear you ask, "But I thought we were writing all these tests so we wouldn't *have* to do QA anymore?" Sorry, but the QA work remains.

The Greatest QA Joke Ever Told:

QA Engineer walks into a bar. Orders a beer. Orders 0 beers. Orders 999999999 beers. Orders a lizard. Orders -1 beers. Orders asfdeljknesv.

When we wrote our tests, we weren't concerning ourselves with anything and everything that could go wrong. Take the search field—we wrote methods for the good and *known* invalid user inputs. There are still plenty of *unknown* invalid user inputs; inputs that might even cause server errors. It's our QA process' job to ferret out those problems. Granted, when those problems are found, our TDD process will kick back in: we'll write a failing test that demonstrates the error, then update the application code so that the test passes.

Load testing

Though our functional tests may be a good start to load testing, we don't have anything in our test suite that's capable of hammering a server. We also need to take special care with load balancing scripts to make sure that we're not adding extra, erroneous data to our production database.

Check out Locust (`http://locust.io/`) if you're looking for a good load testing tool written in Python. Of course, `ab` (Apache Bench, `http://httpd.apache.org/docs/2.2/programs/ab.html`) is still the industry standard.

What shall we build next?

I've been keeping a little list of features that I'd like to see added to JMAD, as we've gone through the book. Here are a few of them that would make for good next steps. If I try them out, I'll try to blog about it (`http://kevinharvey.net/`). If you attempt any of them, or can think of any other good features to add, drop me a line at `hello@kevinharvey.net`.

Authentication for creating solos

We really ought to create user accounts for users who want to add solo information. This would involve not only adding a custom user model, but writing and testing login and logout views. We could also extend authentication to our external API, allowing authenticated activity from third-party applications.

Tagging solos

Solos ought to be able to be tagged with arbitrarily named strings that users can add. Then, users should be able to view a tag and see all the solos tagged with it.

Haystack search

Right now our search function uses the Django ORM directly. `django-haystack` is a venerable project for fine-tuned full text searches. We could start with a simple implementation of the Whoosh backend, then eventually implement faceted search (progressively fine-tuned search by attributes) with a move to Solr.

Celery for caching MusicBrainz data

We're asking a lot of our views to cascade through multiple chained API calls to MusicBrainz and save all of it to the database in a smart way. Why not get the first few in, then queue the rest for later processing with Celery?

An errant data interaction for MusicBrainz

It's possible that we could get erroneous or incomplete data from the MusicBrainz API. We should give our users a way of submitting proposed fixes to that data, and use the MusicBrainz API to submit it to them.

Exposing API documentation with Django REST framework

We've written such nice documentation for our API, it's a shame to squirrel it away in source code. DRF's `DefaultRouter` is one option to expose that documentation via the web. There is also a DRF Swagger project (`https://github.com/marcgibbons/django-rest-swagger`) if you're into JavaScript-y expandables.

To tend or not to tend?

There are competing theories on what to do with a test after you've written it. One school of thought contends that tests are meant to be forgotten. They exist to confirm that the code is still running as it ought to, and there's never really any reason to refactor them later. They either pass or fail, and only need to be changed if they are failing for the wrong reason, or to drive further development. The Django documentation itself encourages this approach.

On the other hand, you could view your test suite as an application to be maintained unto itself. The activities involved might include:

- Keeping your test suite DRY by writing helper methods and subclasses whenever possible
- Optimizing your test suite for speedy runs
- Breaking your test suite into logical chunks that can be run independently

I mostly fall in the latter bracket. I've found test suites to grow to the hundreds of methods, and if it's a drag to run tests or write new ones, you'll quickly find yourself avoiding it.

Fight through the gotchas

Admittedly, I've presented a lot of best-case scenarios as examples, and worked through some of the snarling tracebacks that you can get in the TDD process. You're likely to encounter some nasty ones of your own. Here are a few things to watch out for.

"No module named" errors when using dotted paths to tests

You're not crazy. When you try to run `python manage.py test solos.tests.test_models.SoloTestCase`, how could you possibly get an error like `'solos.tests has no model test_models'`? Of course it has that module, you're looking at it right now! This can crop up when you try to import something that doesn't exist inside one of the modules in the path (most often a class or function that you haven't created yet).

Just run the full test suite for a more helpful error message. This is a good practice anyway when you get a single erroneous test that confuses you.

When error messages get weird, Google is your friend

Output from failed or erroneous tests can be downright ugly, but don't trick yourself into thinking you're the first one to have ever seen it. Be quick to copy and paste confusing error messages directly into your favorite search engine. Many developers have felt your pain, let's just hope they wrote about it in their blog.

Thanks!

I hope you enjoyed reading this book as much as I enjoyed writing it. Drop me a line!

- **Twitter:** @kevinharvey
- hello@kevinharvey.net

Index

A

API
advantages 133
building, with Django REST
    framework 135
data, adding via 147
developer, issues 135
Documentation-Driven testing 134
documentation, writing 134
initial documentation 135-137
using, in application 119
application code
functional test, continuing through 32-36
RequestFactory, used for view
    testing 27-32
search, adding to view 37-48
writing 26
application improvements
better URLs 71
data normalization 71
views 71

B

Betamax
URL 132

C

Continuous Integration (CI) server 6

D

data
adding, via API 147-150

inbound data, validating with
    serializer 150-152
Django admin
activating 95-97
content, adding via 104-108
model list display, configuring 101-104
Django app
setting, for unit tests 23, 24
Django REST framework
about 137
API routing, with DRF's
    SimpleRouter 140-142
automatic APIs, with DRF
    viewsets 142, 143
Django models, converting with
    serializers 144, 145
RetrieveModelMixin, used for
    finishing 146, 147
tests, writing for API endpoints 137-139
URL 137
used, for building API 135
used, for exposing API documentation 158
DRF Swagger project
URL 158
DRY testing 59-61

F

functional test
updating 84-86
functional tests, versus unit tests
about 12
breadth 12
size 12
user, versus developer experience 12

G

get_absolute_url() method 76
Git
  URL 5, 15
gotchas, TDD
  about 159
  Google, using 159
  No module named errors 159

H

Haystack search 158
Homebrew
  URL 13

I

index view
  refactoring 86-91

J

jmad.us project
  about 13
  acceptance criteria 13
  elements, searching with
       WebDriver 20-22
  environment, setting up 13
  functional test, starting 15
  functional test, working 18-20
  initiating 14, 15
  LiveServerTestCase 16
  page, used for opening WebDriver 20
  sample code, obtaining 15
  Selenium 16
  test output, reading 23
  URL 13
  user story, narrating 17, 18

K

key practices, for code writing
  Continuous Integration (CI) 6
  documentation 5
  testing 5
  version control 5

L

ListModelMixin
  URL 144
Locust
  URL 157

M

migration files
  building 83
mock
  about 113-119
  advantages 119, 120
  API calls, encapsulating 122, 123
  API calls, implementing 129, 130
  creating 123-125
  data catching, Celery 158
  MB API, adding to search 120, 121
  pattern, applying to view test 130, 131
  returning, from mock method 125-128
  VCR.py tool 132
MusicBrainz
  about 115
  errant data interaction 158
  sandbox, exploring 115, 118
  URL 115

P

pitfalls
  about 155
  frontend design 156
  load testing 157
  production optimization 155, 156
  quality assurance 156, 157
Python
  URL 13
Python Debugger
  URL 52
  using, in tests 52

R

refactoring
  about 57
  setUpClass, versus setUp 57-59

Thank you for buying
Test-Driven Development with Django

About Packt Publishing

Packt, pronounced 'packed', published its first book, *Mastering phpMyAdmin for Effective MySQL Management*, in April 2004, and subsequently continued to specialize in publishing highly focused books on specific technologies and solutions.

Our books and publications share the experiences of your fellow IT professionals in adapting and customizing today's systems, applications, and frameworks. Our solution-based books give you the knowledge and power to customize the software and technologies you're using to get the job done. Packt books are more specific and less general than the IT books you have seen in the past. Our unique business model allows us to bring you more focused information, giving you more of what you need to know, and less of what you don't.

Packt is a modern yet unique publishing company that focuses on producing quality, cutting-edge books for communities of developers, administrators, and newbies alike. For more information, please visit our website at www.packtpub.com.

About Packt Open Source

In 2010, Packt launched two new brands, Packt Open Source and Packt Enterprise, in order to continue its focus on specialization. This book is part of the Packt Open Source brand, home to books published on software built around open source licenses, and offering information to anybody from advanced developers to budding web designers. The Open Source brand also runs Packt's Open Source Royalty Scheme, by which Packt gives a royalty to each open source project about whose software a book is sold.

Writing for Packt

We welcome all inquiries from people who are interested in authoring. Book proposals should be sent to author@packtpub.com. If your book idea is still at an early stage and you would like to discuss it first before writing a formal book proposal, then please contact us; one of our commissioning editors will get in touch with you.

We're not just looking for published authors; if you have strong technical skills but no writing experience, our experienced editors can help you develop a writing career, or simply get some additional reward for your expertise.

Web Development with Django Cookbook

ISBN: 978-1-78328-689-8   Paperback: 294 pages

Over 70 practical recipes to create multilingual, responsive, and scalable websites with Django

1. Improve your skills by developing models, forms, views, and templates.

2. Create a rich user experience using Ajax and other JavaScript techniques.

3. A practical guide to writing and using APIs to import or export data.

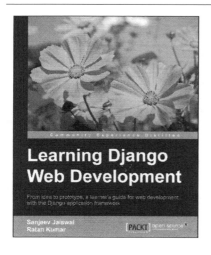

Learning Django Web Development

ISBN: 978-1-78398-440-4   Paperback: 336 pages

From idea to prototype, a learner's guide for web development with the Django application framework

1. Build two real-life based projects, one based on SQL and other based on NoSQL.

2. Best practices to code, debug, and deploy the Django web application.

3. Easy to follow instructions and real world examples to build highly effective Django web application.

Please check **www.PacktPub.com** for information on our titles

Django Essentials

ISBN: 978-1-78398-370-4   Paperback: 172 pages

Develop simple web applications with the powerful Django framework

1. Get to know MVC pattern and the structure of Django.

2. Create your first webpage with Django mechanisms.

3. Enable user interaction with forms.

AngularJS Test-driven Development

ISBN: 978-1-78439-883-5   Paperback: 206 pages

Implement the best practices to improve your AngularJS applications using test-driven development

1. Learn about TDD techniques, the TDD lifecycle, and its power through clear examples to enhance your Angular applications.

2. Integrate AngularJS testing using Karma and Protractor to perform JavaScript unit tests.

3. A practical guide filled with examples that focus on a wide range of testing techniques with AngularJS components.

Please check **www.PacktPub.com** for information on our titles

Made in the USA
Lexington, KY
05 October 2015